A Breath
of
Fresh Prayer

John Evans

Pray!

Colossians 4:2

John H. Evans

A Breath
of
Fresh Prayer

John H. Evans

FOURTH PRINTING

To contact the author, write to:
Dr. John H. Evans
c/o Grace Church
P.O. Box 3311
Sierra Vista, Arizona 85636

PUBLISHED BY:
BRENTWOOD CHRISTIAN PRESS
4000 BEALLWOOD AVENUE
COLUMBUS, GEORGIA 31904

This book is dedicated in loving memory of:
Eileen C. Evans, my mother
John H. Evans, Sr., my father
Clay M. Lind, my father-in-law
Dr. Gwyn Walters, my mentor

"Precious in the sight of the Lord is the death of his saints."
Psalm 116:15

And in loving tribute to:
Lydia Alice Lind, my mother-in-law

CONTENTS

If you will take just a moment to scan the Table of Contents, you will discover that there are thirty-one chapters, a month's worth of reading. You may wish to read this book in several sittings or take bite-sized chunks of one chapter a day for each day of the month.

May God bless you as you read, and may God raise up in you another person of prayer for the praise of His glory.

ACKNOWLEDGMENTS

It has been said, "Scholarship is one man standing on the shoulders of another." Whatever knowledge may be found in this book I owe to all my teachers who have gone before me. I have been blessed by my studies at Wheaton College (Illinois) and at Gordon-Conwell Theological Seminary (South Hamilton, Massachusetts). In particular, at Gordon-Conwell, it was my great privilege to sit under the teaching and preaching of the late Dr. Gwyn Walters, Professor of Ministry. Of even greater influence in my life than his preaching on prayer was his practice of prayer. He rose early every day to meet with God. Even after many a late night and having worked his finger to the bone, he still got up for that morning meeting. I soon came to realize the secret to the power that attended his preaching. It was his sincere and utter devotion to Jesus Christ expressed by his prayer life. Powerful preaching came out of his powerful praying. Furthermore, Dr. Walters lived his sermons. In his preparation for preaching he lived with the text, by the text, and up to the text, and he covered it all with prayer. It was Thomas Fuller, M.D. who wrote in GNOMOLOGIA (1732): "None can pray well but he that lives well."

I also wish to acknowledge all the authors of books and articles on prayer that I have read across the years. Many of their names are now forgotten, but their lessons linger. In whatever ways I may have borrowed from them, I acknowledge my deep indebtedness. And so, I thank God for all the teachers, preachers, authors and practitioners of prayer, who have taught me of prayer: its importance and its power.

Of course, this book would never have been written without the love, encouragement and prayer support of my family and of my Grace Church family. How greatly blessed of God I am to be in a praying family and church!

I am most grateful to God for the weekly fellowship in prayer with other praying pastors and ministry leaders over the past seven years. They have shown themselves to be "faithful in prayer" (Romans 12:12). I thank God for each of you:

Mr. Brayton Back, Rev. Michael Bergman,
Dr. Gene Boone, Rev. Shawn Buckhanan,
Rev. Charles Carlson, Rev. Dwight Collins,
Mr. Charles Denler, Rev. William Dwyer,
Rev. James Fogarty, Rev. Pete Hawker, Dr. James Hoston,
Rev. Norbert Kinney, Rev. David Kurek,
Rev. James Matthias, Rev. Clea McCaa,
Rev. Andy MacFarlane, Rev. Rick McEver,
Rev. Arthur Mimnaugh, Rev. Brent Nicola,
Rev. Arthur Parson, Dr. Atticus Register,
Rev. Edward Schaeffer, Rev. Thomas Sears,
Mr. Jim Sutherland, Dr. Joseph Tumpkin,
Rev. Robert Waldron, and Rev. Randy Youngblood.

I wish to express my sincere gratitude to Shirley Cain who typed and re-typed this manuscript many times for publication. In addition, my heart was greatly stirred when I learned that she made the commitment to pray twenty minutes daily while typing chapter 25! And to all who attended "the proof-reading party" I give you my heartfelt thanks. They are as follows:

Dr. Thomas Askew, Karen Bolton, Jaimie Bolton,
Sean Bratton, Marlaina Bratton, Dick Claxton,
Judy Claxton, Joan Evans, Robyn Gray, Jill Landon,
Renee Levesque, Meghan Jeffers, Mairen Jeffers,
Bill Moore, Cyndy Moore, George Page,
Maxine Page, David Smith, Bobbie Smith,
Sterling Wasden, and Millie Wasden.

Finally, a special thank you to my wife, Joanie, for her extra effort in proof reading.

John Evans
Antelope Run
Sierra Vista, Arizona
July 2000

PREFACE

Samuel Chadwick wrote, "The one concern of the devil is to keep Christians from praying. He fears nothing from prayerless studies, prayerless work, and prayerless religion. He laughs at our toil, mocks at our wisdom, but trembles when we pray."

My purpose in writing this book is to motivate you, as a Christian, to pray and to keep on praying. The reason is that many prayers mean many answers, many thanks, and many praises to our God.

There is a great deal of talk in Christian circles today about prayer. There are many fine books on prayer. There are seminars, workshops and a variety of audio and visual aids all designed to teach us about prayer.

However, this is not a book on "how" (the mechanics of prayer) to pray. Nor is it chiefly a book about the "power" (the dynamics of prayer), although inspiring, true-to-life stories of answered prayer are included here. Also, it does not fully address the question of "what" (the specifics of prayer) we are to pray for. It is, rather, a book written to get you on your knees, or on your feet, in prayer; to get you out of your chair and into prayer. I say "on your feet" because for eighteen hundred years Christians prayed standing up! The most common physical posture in prayer was the 'Victory Position.' In taking their place at prayer, Christians stood with their arms raised heavenward.

My heart's desire is to have you, the reader, moved from thinking about prayer, reading about prayer (including this book!), and talking about prayer, to praying.

In keeping with this, the most important page in this book is *136*. Please resist the temptation to turn there now. Let's save the best for last.

"Devote yourselves to prayer, being watchful and thankful."
Colossians 4:2, New International Version

Chapter 1

THE MOST IMPORTANT THING
I WILL DO TODAY

The most important thing I will do today is **PRAY**!

"Only ask, and I will give you the nations as your inheritance, the ends of the earth as your possession."
Psalm 2:8, New Living Translation

Chapter 2

PRAYER FROM A "LAND ROVER"

Africa ...The Dark Continent ... dark in the sense of hidden from our eyes. But darker still are those "who are darkened in their understanding and separated from the life of God because of the ignorance that is in them due to the hardening of their hearts" (Ephesians 4:18).

Driving along on a bone-jarring mountain road in Africa, a missionary, his heart filled to the brim with the expansive love of God for lost people, looked out the bug-and-mud-splattered windshield of his Land Rover at the valley below. What he saw brought his heart to the breaking point. There, camped below, as far as the eye could see, were thousands upon thousands of refugees from the civil war in the Belgian Congo.

At that moment it was not time that seemed to stand still, but the air. Motionless ... hot ... dry ... without even the whisper of a breeze. And then there were all those cooking fires. Fire and smoke, blended together with filtered sunlight, formed mushroom-shaped clouds above.

Knowing full well that every cooking fire represented a village full of people, our missionary called out to heaven and said, "Oh God, what's to become of all those people?" His mind, cluttered with thoughts of the demands of the day, was clear now. All he could think about was their lack of the love of God and the knowledge of Christ.

And then, from inside the cabin of that all-terrain vehicle, he heard a voice, clear and strong. A voice that spoke impeccable English and said, "Ask me for them!"

This poor Baptist missionary didn't have a clue as to what he should do with this. There was no body attached to the voice.

13

It should be noted here that our missionary was no stranger to the mission field. He was a veteran of some twenty-five years of service. And being of sound mind, he paid no attention to the voice and continued on his way.

A short while later, still burdened by the sight of all those lost people, he cried out again, "Oh God, what's to become of all those people?" Then a second time he heard the voice...that same, clear, unmistakable voice... speaking to him from the vacant passenger seat, "Ask me for them!"

Immediately he pulled his vehicle over to the side of the road. "Whew!" he said. "That's the kind of thing God would say if God were to speak."

As he sat there collecting his thoughts, he reasoned that this is how God acted in the Old Testament. He remembered the story of the boy Samuel in the Temple who in the middle of the night heard a voice saying, "Samuel! Samuel!" He further reasoned that God had indeed done this kind of thing in the past, but this is not the middle of the night, and his name is not Samuel. And as a biblical literalist, he could disregard this voice speaking to him.

But still he struggled with his thoughts, rehearsing in his mind what he had just perceived to be the voice of God. Thinking again that what he had heard was the kind of thing God would say, he asked himself, "What exactly had God said?" "Ask me for them!"

Finally, he came to terms with himself and decided that he could, in good faith, offer a prayer to God and not violate his theological convictions. So he prayed, "Lord, for Jesus' sake, give me the souls of the people in this valley."

Even as he prayed he thought of how he might possibly explain all of this to his Baptist brothers. He would have to discern if this were of God or not, and he would have to do it by some test, because that's the rule in the Baptist tradition. He shouldn't take anything as being directly from God without checking it out against Scripture and against reality.

And so he said, "Lord, if this is you, and you want me to spend more time in this valley evangelizing these people, I'll go right down there and preach. If anyone shows interest or responds, then I'll return here."

"There," he said, "that'll do it, because I won't have to tell anyone I heard this voice. If there is a response down there, I won't have to tell them how I got there. I can just tell them I found some people, I preached, and they were saved."

The missionary cranked up the engine of that old Land Rover and headed for the valley below. Upon arriving at the very first village, he preached the good news of Jesus Christ. At the close of his message eleven adults, on their first hearing of the gospel, received Christ as their Savior.

That missionary said, "Whew! This place is ready." After that he went back again and again. In the space of five years sixty new churches were planted.

Three years later, by 1980, twenty more churches had been planted. Wonder of wonders, in less than eight years 80 new congregations of the Lord had been established. These new believers were studying the Scriptures, worshipping the Lord, requesting Christian baptism, and sending out missionaries of their own.

The missionary never shared this story with his Baptist friends as long as he lived. He did, however, share it with Dr. Carl George of Fuller Theological Seminary (Pasadena, California) before he died. After his death Dr. George shared it with those Baptist brothers. Do you know what they said? "So that's what happened there. We wondered about that because that's a good work. That work is still going on over there. They're still planting more churches from those churches. God was involved in all of that."

There are, of course, many lessons that can be learned from this true story: lessons about ... vision, the harvest, risk-taking, faith, testing, and prayer. Let's consider the importance of prayer in all of this.

The apostle James wrote, "You do not have because you do not ask God. When you ask, you do not receive, because you ask with wrong motives, that you may spend what you get on your pleasures" (James 4: 2-3). At the core of all true prayer there is this matter of asking ... asking God. Whether it is a recitation of the Lord's Prayer or listening to a child's bedtime prayer, asking is central.

Jesus himself, in the greatest sermon ever preached, addressed the importance of what I call *asking prayer*. "Ask and it will be given to you; seek and you will find; knock and the door will be opened to you. For everyone who asks receives; he who seeks finds, and to him who knocks the door will be opened" (Matthew 7:7-8).

What if our Baptist missionary had refused to ask God for those people? What would he have been left with? In the second Psalm God the Father addressing his Son says, "Ask of me, and I will make the nations your inheritance, the ends of the earth your possession" (Psalm 2:8). Jesus asked. The Father gave. You and I (and the church) are the beneficiaries.

Little did our Baptist missionary realize that sultry afternoon on a mountain road that the most important thing he would do that day would be to pray.

Have you prayed today?

Notes

"My house shall be called a house of prayer."
– Jesus
Matthew 21:13, New King James Version

Chapter 3

A PASSION FOR PRAYER

A passion for prayer comes out of a passion for Christ. The more passionate you are in your love for Christ, the more passionate you will be about prayer. This passion cannot be taught, transferred, or manufactured. It is only caught as you reach out and experience all "the extravagant dimensions of Christ's love" (Ephesians 3:16-19). It will happen when you are filled through all your being with the love of God himself.

As your love for God deepens, it will excite your passion for him. The love that arouses this passion for God can only be imparted by the Holy Spirit. II Timothy 1:7 says, "For God has not given us a spirit of fear, but a spirit of power and *love* and a sound mind" (J.B. Phillips translation). So let your heart stay open to fresh fillings and fresh feelings of God's love as he pours them out by his Holy Spirit.

In the year 49 AD the Christians in Rome were so passionate about their love for Jesus and so powerful in their witness that the Emperor Claudius expelled all the Jews from Rome, thinking that they were all followers of Christ!

To paraphrase another writer, can you think of anyone who loves you more, understands you better, or believes in you more than anyone in this world, than Jesus? The perfect love of Jesus for us and our undying love for Him ought to draw us to him in passionate prayer.

Something of this passion after God was captured in a heart-wrenching scene in the film "Shadowlands" (1993), when the twentieth century's greatest Christian apologist, C.S. Lewis, found out that his beloved wife's cancer was in remission. An Anglican priest at Oxford University commiserated with him: "I know how hard you've been praying. And now God is answering you."

Lewis replied, "That's not why I pray, Harry. I pray because I can't help myself. I pray because I'm helpless. I pray because the need flows out of me all the time, waking and sleeping. It doesn't change God. It changes me."

C.S. Lewis spoke of prayer rising out of his innermost being that had transforming power in his life. Of course, one can be passionate or passive about one's faith. For example, it was reported in a recent Gallup Poll that only ten percent of Americans have "transforming faith," meaning that it makes a discernible difference in their lives.

Jesus demonstrated his passion for God, his passion for prayer, when he did some spring housecleaning at the temple. With whip in hand, he scattered the coins of the moneychangers, overturning their tables. He said, "It is written, my house will be called a house of prayer, but you are making it a den of robbers" (Matthew 21:13). Upon hearing these words and witnessing this scene, Jesus' disciples remembered that it was written, "Zeal for your house will consume me" (John 2:17). Our Lord was eaten up with a holy passion for God and for the things of God, namely, prayer.

John Piper, a Baptist minister in Minneapolis, Minnesota wrote about two great passions in the universe: God's passion to be glorified and man's passion to be satisfied. However, the two do not need to be in conflict he said. They can come to simultaneous fulfillment through worship because God is most glorified in me when I am most satisfied in him alone.

Prayer is just such a spiritual act of worship. Whatever else we may say about prayer, the overarching reason why we are to pray with such passion is so that Jesus may bring glory to the Father: not to get our prayers answered, not to receive comfort, etc. Jesus said, "And I will do whatever you ask in my name, so that the Son may bring glory to the Father. You may ask me for anything in my name, and I will do it" (John 14:13-14).

When it comes to prayer, just how passionate are you?

Notes

"We shall devote ourselves whole-heartedly
to prayer and the ministry of the Word."
Acts 6:4, J. B. Phillips Translation

Chapter 4

PRAYER AS PRIORITY

The most important thing I will do today is pray. Whatever else I may or may not accomplish today, I shall have succeeded in doing what is most important. Importance speaks of great worth and significance. Everything else comes up short by comparison.

You have heard it said that, "The main thing is the main thing is the main thing." What then is the main thing? It's "THE MAIN THING!" No, dear reader, I have not lost my mind. I simply wish to emphasize that the main thing is the most important thing. It's the chief thing. It's what we call our priority. Priority is the importance you give to something.

As Christians, prayer is to be our priority. It is to be first in the order of things. Take, for example, the practice of prayer in the Early Church. From the very beginning, prayer was their priority.

As the young Church increased in number it experienced growing pains. A problem arose concerning the daily distribution of food baskets to widows in the church. The number of Greek-speaking Jewish widows, dependent on relief from the church, had become disproportionately large. As such, they were not receiving their fair share of the food. Grumbling broke out in the church at Jerusalem and threatened the fellowship of the believers. The matter was so serious that the Twelve (apostles) issued a call for a congregational meeting.

In proposing a solution, the apostles first of all recognized that there is a difference of ministry based on the distribution of gifts to the body of Christ by the Holy Spirit. Broadly speaking, they understood two categories of gifts: speaking and serving (I Peter 4:11). The apostles were called and gifted to preach (speaking gift). Nothing was to interfere with that. And so they proposed that seven spiritually-minded and empowered men be given the responsibility of looking after the practical needs of the church (serving gift).

It is important that we take careful notice of the apostles' exact words at this point. "We will turn this responsibility over to them (i.e. the newly elected deacons) and (we) will *give our attention to prayer and the ministry of the word*" (Acts 6:4). Praying and preaching. That was the divine order for the apostles. Prayer was to come first. Prayer was the foundation stone for ministry. The word for "attention" in Acts 6:4 means to adhere firmly to, persist in, remain devoted to. Making prayer the priority for life and ministry was characteristic of the Early Church.

Turning again to the Book of Acts, we discover that the vitality of the first Christians was to be seen in their devotion to prayer. After the ascension of our Lord to heaven, the disciples of Jesus returned to Jerusalem from the Mount of Olives. The Scripture describes the scene. "When they arrived, they went upstairs to the room where they were staying. Those present were Peter, John, James and Andrew, Philip and Thomas, Bartholomew and Matthew, James, son of Alphaeus and Simon the Zealot, and Judas, son of James. They all joined together *constantly in prayer*, along with the women and Mary, the mother of Jesus, and with his brothers" (Acts 1:13-14).

Ten days. Ten days of prayer. Ten days of waiting and worshipping. They agreed that they were in this for the long haul, completely devoted to prayer. On the day of Pentecost when the Holy Spirit arrived the believers, now numbering about a hundred and twenty, were in the posture of prayer. This devotion to prayer continued throughout those formative years of the young and growing church. Whenever the church gathered, "they *devoted* themselves to the apostles' teaching and to the fellowship, to the breaking of bread and to *prayer*" (Acts 2:42). The word for "devoted" here is from the same verb that is translated "constantly" (in prayer) in Acts 1:14. The believers continued steadfastly in their prayers to God.

This *prayoritizing* carried over in the church at Rome, where the apostle Paul speaks of their faith as being talked about all over the world. He reminds them to "Be joyful in hope, patient in affliction, *faithful in prayer*" (Romans 12:12). In other words, the apostle is saying, keep on doing what you've been doing, finding your joy in the Lord at all times, enduring hardships, and attending constantly to prayer.

Paul brings this same, strong emphasis to prayer as priority in writing to the church at Colossae. "*Devote yourselves to prayer*, being watchful and thankful" (Colossians 4:2). As in all our previous references regarding devotion to prayer, we encounter the same Greek verb for giving attention to prayer. Surely you can tell where someone's priority lies by observing the time and attention he or she gives to prayer.

The paramount importance of prayer is found in this exhortation to the Christians at Philippi. "Do not be anxious about anything, but *in everything, by prayer* and petition, with thanksgiving, present your requests to God" (Philippians 4:6). Anxious for nothing ... prayerful for everything ... and thankful for anything. At the heart of these three enjoinders we are instructed that everything is to be brought to God in prayer. Everything.

Furthermore, God's answer to anxiety is prayer. Whenever anxious thoughts begin to multiply ... pray. The fact that we are told to pray about everything is a convincing statement of the place that prayer should have in our lives. The message here is clear. Prayer as priority. PRAYER BEFORE ANYTHING ELSE.

Once I was invited to have lunch with a pastor who was visiting from out of town. I was told beforehand that he had been very successful in seeing many people added to his church through his efforts in private evangelism. So devoted was he in presenting the gospel that he managed to eat his lunch at his desk in just seven minutes every day. This allowed him more time to tell others the good news of the gospel.

Over some slices of pizza the subject of prayer was broached. I shared some of my thoughts about devotion to prayer and the conversation fell silent. After an awkward pause, our visiting pastor spoke. He expressed amazement that one would give prayer such a place of prominence in his life. He then candidly told me prayer had no such place in his life. After all, he wouldn't want to give the impression to his congregation that he was lazy! He thought of prayer as idle inactivity. Prayer was what one did if he had nothing better to do.

This man was making converts *to* Christ, but was he making disciples *of* Christ? Would he be teaching these new Christians, by precept and example, the place that prayer should have in their lives? With few exceptions, the prayer life of a congregation seldom rises above that of its pastor.

As we think together along the lines of *prayer as priority*, consider the psalmist David, Israel's most illustrious king. David told us what his priority was in life. In Psalm 109:4 he declared, "I am a man of prayer." Whatever else may be remembered about David (e.g. "a man after God's own heart"), he was a man of prayer.

In a psalm having to do with morning prayers David wrote, "*In the morning*, O Lord, you hear my voice; in the morning I lay my requests before you and wait in expectation" (Psalm 5:3). David prayed first thing in the morning. Prayer was his priority. He gave the first part, the freshest part, the finest part of his day to God.

God desires to hear our voice in prayer in the morning. If prayer is not taken care of in the morning, the demands of the day and the cares of this life can easily squeeze out the time for it. Taking time for prayer is taking time for God, taking time with God. None of us can "make time." We can only take a portion of the same time that is allotted to all of us to get alone with God in the fellowship of prayer. Why should anyone else hear your voice in the morning until God has heard it first? It was the world-renowned Baptist minister Dr. W. A. Criswell who was quoted as having said, "Keep your mornings for God!"

According to Psalm 63 David sought the Lord early. "O, God, you are my God, *early* will I seek you; my soul thirsts for you, my flesh longs for you, in a dry and thirsty land where there is no water" (Psalm 63:1, New King James Version).

Would you like to be at your spiritual best in something? To excel? To go to the top? To go over the top? Let me explain. An anagram is a word or phrase formed from another word or phrase by transposing or rearranging letters. Take, for example, the word "PRESBYTERIAN." Using only the letters in this word and not using any letter more than once, you can spell out "BEST IN PRAYER." Are Presbyterians really best in prayer? I don't know. You may wish to ask one! But that's not the point here. The point is that it doesn't matter what your denomination is or isn't ... you can be best in prayer. If you are seeking to excel in prayer, you can. If you are to be the best in prayer, you must bow in prayer.

Perhaps you remember the news story about Alicia Chapman, a school bus driver in Miami, telling how she remained calm as her bus, full of disabled children, was held hostage for seventy-five minutes by a hijacker. When asked how she was able to hold herself together during that ordeal she said, "I pray a lot." Here is a woman who has made prayer a priority in her life.

In the final analysis, of course, we Christians pray because we are commanded to pray. It's simply a matter of obedience. An obedient Christian is a praying Christian. As the Scripture says, "Therefore, let everyone who is godly offer prayer to you while you may be found; surely when the mighty waters rise, they will not reach him" (Psalm 32:6). And again, following our Lord's directive, "When you pray, go into your room, close the door and pray to your Father who is unseen" (Matthew 6:6). Jesus did not say *if* you pray. He said, "*when* you pray." Sharpening his stylus, the apostle Paul gets right to the point: "Pray continually" (I Thessalonians 5:17). Christians are to pray at all times and never stop praying. Praying is like breathing. Although one is natural and the other supernatural, both must be done. Breathing will enable you to survive. Praying will enable you to thrive!

A Korean woman once said to me, "If the first button isn't right, everything else will be wrong." Applied to the spiritual disciplines, prayer is the first button. If you "button up" with prayer each and every day, making prayer your priority, the other disciplines of the Christian life will fall in line.

Our daughter Joy has found a novel way of continuing in the discipline of prayer. She writes out her prayers like love letters to God.

On my desk where I'm writing this chapter sits an inexpensive plastic sign. I had it made locally at a sign shop. Engraved in white letters against a brilliant red background, it is a visual reminder to me of my spiritual priority. It reads: THE MOST IMPORTANT THING I WILL DO TODAY IS PRAY.

Excuse me while I close the door behind me. Jesus is calling. It's time to pray.

Notes

"Come near to God and God will come near to you."
James 4:8, New Century Version

Chapter 5

A BREATH OF FRESH PRAYER

There is nothing quite like a breath of fresh prayer. Consider this classic description of prayer.

> "Prayer is the soul's sincere desire,
> uttered or unexpressed;
> The motion of a hidden fire
> that trembles in the breast.
>
> Prayer is the burden of a sigh,
> the falling of a tear;
> The upward glancing of an eye,
> when none but God is near."
>
> *What Is Prayer?* (Stanza 1)
> by James Montgomery (1771-1854)

The first mention of prayer in the Bible is recorded in Genesis 4:26. "At that time men began to call on the name of the Lord." Prayer, in essence, is calling upon the name of the Lord.

The last mention of prayer is found in Revelation 22:20. Our Lord, speaking in reference to his return, says, "Yes, I am coming soon." The venerable apostle John, writing under the inspiration of the Holy Spirit, prays on behalf of the church when he writes, "Amen. Come, Lord Jesus." The Bible opens as it closes...with people calling upon the name of the Lord. And in all the books in between we find men and women at prayer.

I heard the story of a man who was driving through an intersection one day and his four-year old son was in the car with him. The car door flew open and the little boy rolled out of the vehicle right into the middle of traffic which was coming from four directions. The last thing the father saw was a set of car wheels, moving at a very fast rate of speed, just about on top of his son. All he knew to do was cry, "JESUS!"

As soon as the father could bring his car to a halt, he jumped out and ran to his son who was perfectly all right. The man driving the car that had almost hit the child was absolutely hysterical. The father went over to him and tried to comfort him. "Man, don't be upset," he said. "My son is all right. He's okay. Don't be concerned about it. Just thank God you were able to stop!"

"You don't understand!" the man responded. "I never touched my brakes!"

Here prayer might be defined as calling out the name of the Lord in a moment of crisis. There are, of course, many good definitions of prayer. A devout praying pastor friend of mine, Dr. Joseph Tumpkin, has offered the following:

"Prayer is a dialogue between the living God and one who has been touched by His grace."

"A loving conversation with God."

"Prayer is the vital breath of spiritual life, the divinely appointed means of fellowship with the Almighty."

Here is my definition of prayer: Prayer (in its simplest and purest form) is speaking with God, face-to-face, as a man would speak with his friend. It is communion with the Lord in your heart.

I base this on the account in Exodus 33:7-11 where Moses, a man of God, would pitch a tent outside the camp of Israel. It was called the "Tent of Meeting." Anyone who felt the need to inquire of the Lord about a matter would go to this tent. When Moses went into the tent, a pillar of cloud would come down and hover at the entrance while the Lord spoke with Moses. This "face-to-face" encounter with God meant that Moses was in the very presence of the Almighty, and there was direct communication between them.

Prayer is a gracious privilege for those of us who truly believe in God. Prayer is the usher that escorts us into his presence. In prayer, we are drawing near to God. As the writer to the Hebrews put it, "Therefore, brothers, since we have confidence to enter the Most Holy Place by the blood of Jesus, by a new and living way opened for us through the curtain, that is his body, and since we have a great priest over the house of God, let us *draw near* to God with a sincere heart in full assurance of faith, having our hearts sprinkled to cleanse us from a guilty con- science and having our bodies washed with pure water" (Hebrews 10:19-22). Either we are drawing near to God or we are drifting away from God. To draw near to God is to come close to him. It is to be in fellowship with God, or as the apostle James implored, "Come near to God and he will come near to you" (James 4:8). It has been said, "If you don't feel close to God, guess who moved!"

Let's close this chapter by listing ten benefits of prayer.

1. It is a daily reminder of our need for God and our dependence upon Him. (As a friend once said to me, "God can live his life without me, but I can't live my life without God.")
2. It serves to heighten our awareness of God.
3. It helps us to center our thoughts upon God rather than upon the circumstances of our life.
4. It helps us to look for God in everything that happens in our lives.
5. It increases our faith as we see prayer answered.
6. It gives power to our Christian witness.
7. It invigorates the soul, energizing us.
8. It develops our intimacy with the Lord.
9. It distributes peace to us.
10. It is the means of fellowship with God.

"Rising early in the morning long before daylight,
He left and went out to a lonely spot and prayed there."
Mark 1:35, The Berkeley Version

Chapter 6

THE PRAYER LIFE OF JESUS

When it comes to prayer, Jesus is our role model. He practiced what he preached to others. "And when you pray, do not be like the hypocrites, for they love to pray standing in the synagogues and on the street corners to be seen by men. I tell you the truth, they have received their reward in full. But when you pray, go into your room, close the door and pray to your Father who is unseen. Then your Father, who sees what is done in secret, will reward you. And when you pray, do not keep on babbling like pagans, for they think they will be heard because of their many words. Do not be like them, for your Father knows what you need before you ask him" (Matthew 6:5-8).

Having said this, our Lord then proceeded to give his disciples a pattern prayer, commonly referred to as 'The Lord's Prayer.' That, however, is a misnomer. It would be better called 'The Disciples' Prayer.' In this prayer Jesus gave an example of how we as believers should pray (Matthew 6:9-13).

Jesus made prayer the priority for his life and ministry. He prayed in private (Mark 1:35) as well as in public (John 11:41-42). In one of his public prayers Jesus prayed for himself, for his disciples, and for all believers (John 17).

"Jesus Our Role Model"

It is worth noting the times and occasions when Jesus prayed. He prayed:

At his baptism	Luke 3:21-22
Very early in the morning	Mark 1:35
In lonely places	Luke 5:16

35

At the tomb of Lazarus	John 11:41-42
In public	John 17
On a mountainside	Matthew 14:23
For little children	Matthew 19:13-15
A night spent in prayer before making one of the most important decisions of his life: choosing his disciples.	Luke 6:12-16
With Peter, James, and John on a mountain	Luke 9:28-29
In a garden called Gethsemane	Matthew 26:36-46
We even have a mention of Jesus praying for Peter, although we don't know exactly when that took place	Luke 22:31-32
On the cross	Matthew 27:45-46; Luke 23:34; 23:44-46
The healing of a deaf and dumb man	Mark 7:31-35
The healing of a boy with an evil spirit	Mark 9:29
In private	Luke 9:18
Jesus praying in a certain place	Luke 11:1
At the Last Supper	Luke 22:19
The feeding of the 5,000	Mark 6:41
On the road to Emmaus	Luke 24:30
A prayer of blessing at his ascension	Luke 24:50

Jesus established once and for all the importance of daily prayer. In his private life and for the sake of his public ministry, Jesus devoted himself to prayer. It was his habit. Just as it was his custom to attend services in the synagogue every Sabbath (Luke 4:16), so it was his practice to pray at the beginning of each new day. "*Very early in the morning,* while it was still dark, Jesus got up, left the house and went off to a solitary place, where *he prayed*" (Mark 1:35).

This praying took place on a Sunday morning in the winter of 28 AD. The day before was the Jewish Sabbath. On that day Jesus taught in the synagogue, drove out an evil spirit, healed Peter's mother-in-law of a fever, and enjoyed an afternoon meal with his disciples. That evening after sunset, with the whole town gathered at the door, Jesus ministered to the sick and demon-possessed. After a day that was certainly physically, emotionally and spiritually taxing, it was then that Jesus rose up before the sun to pray. Matthew Henry comments, "Though as God he was prayed to, as man he prayed."

One cold, dark Easter morning my alarm clock, named appropriately "Shake Awake," rudely roused my wife and me from our peaceful slumber. I lay there like a hibernating bear, not wanting to leave my warm, comfortable den. My wife rolled over and whispered to me, "It's so hard to get up in the morning." And in that moment this thought crossed my mind: "Yes, but He (Jesus) got up in the morning for you." Oh, did he ever! Easter day!

"Evening, morning and noon, I cry out...and he hears my voice" (Psalm 55:17). Saturate your life, your day, with prayer. Of course, our praying is not to be limited to the morning only. *Anytime* is the perfect time to pray.

For us as Christians, Jesus is our perfect role model. He prayed first thing in the morning. It is in the morning when we are at our freshest, when we can give our best to God. Sincere, heart-felt prayer to God as the sun splits the horizon, acknowledging our deep, personal dependence upon him, will set our course for the day.

There is no substitute for prayer. And there are no shortcuts to it either. Daily prayer requires daily discipline. The discipline of prayer is a part of the cost of being a disciple.

The Scripture underscores the need to keep your priorities straight. In Ecclesiastes 11:6 we read, "Sow your seed *in the morning*, and at evening let not your hands be idle, for you do not know which will succeed, whether this or that, or whether both will do equally well." Why do this? Because we don't know what a day will bring forth or what tomorrow holds.

"Prayer should be the key of the morning...the lock of
the evening."

Owen Tellhan (1620).

"Prayer will never do our work for us. What it will do is
to strengthen us for work which must be done."

Author Unknown

The writer to the Hebrews encapsulates for us the prayer life
of Jesus. "During the days of Jesus' life on earth, he offered up
prayers and petitions with loud cries and tears to the One who
could save him from death, and he was heard because of his rev-
erent submission" (Hebrews 5:7).

Our Lord's ministry of intercession continues for us to this
very day. Jesus himself, during this present age, is spending his
time interceding for us according to the will of the Father.
"Therefore he is able to save completely those who come to God
through him, because he always lives to intercede for them"
(Hebrews 7:25).

We are most like Jesus when we do what Jesus did. Jesus
prayed frequently and fervently. Do you want to be like Jesus?
Then pray.

Notes

"When you seek me, you shall find me;
if you search with all your heart,
I will let you find me, says the Lord."
Jeremiah 29:13-14, New English Bible

Chapter 7

PURPOSE IN PRAYER

Prayer is about relationship. It's about drawing near, coming close to God. One of the great purposes of prayer is to deepen our relationship with God. "Then you will call upon me and come and pray to me, and I will listen to you. You will seek me and find me when you seek me with all your heart. I will be found by you, declares the Lord" (Jeremiah 29:12-14). In fact, prayer grows out of a relationship with God as our Father. When the disciples of Jesus asked him to teach them to pray, Jesus said, "When you pray, say, "Father ..."" (Luke 11:1-2).

Prayer is one of the gracious means God has appointed for us to grow in our relationship to him. Prayer is about spending time with the One who loves you and the One whom you love, so as to deepen that love relationship. When Karl Barth, a world-renown German theologian and one of the greatest theological thinkers in the Christian church during the last 300 years, was asked what he had learned after a lifetime of study in the Bible and theology, he replied, "Jesus loves me this I know, for the Bible tells me so."

In the Christian's earthly life there are essentially three stages: birth, growth, and maturity. Prayer enables us to grow towards maturity, which is, in essence, our sanctification.

Prayer provides us with access to God through whom we may seek Christ, who is, in fact, the grand object of our prayers. Above all else, in our prayers we ought to seek Jesus: nothing more, nothing less, and nothing else. "Since then, you have been raised with Christ, set your hearts on things above, where Christ is seated at the right hand of God" (Colossians 3:1).

Like Isaiah the prophet, when we come into the presence of God as weak, sinful humans, our first thought is: I'm going to die! (Isaiah 6:5). Then we are overcome with the thought of what an awesome privilege it is to be in the very presence of God.

As a first year seminary student I was challenged in chapel by a visiting pastor to make it my aim, above all else, to cultivate my personal relationship with Jesus Christ. I discovered early on that prayer, private and consistent, would lead me into a greater intimacy with Jesus Christ than I had ever known before. A survey of Scripture brought me to a new understanding of intimacy with God. God has no favorites, but he does have intimates.

Consider the following. On the day of Pentecost about 3,000 new believers were added to the church. Prior to that occasion, we read of more than 500 brothers who saw the risen Christ in His glorified body (I Corinthians 15:6). In the Upper Room the believers numbered about a 120 (Acts 1:15). Luke, the historian, makes mention of our Lord appointing 72 others who were sent out two by two. Matthew lists for us the names of the 12 disciples Jesus called to himself. Mark writes about 4 prominent disciples: Peter, James, John, and Andrew. This quartet enjoyed a private meeting with our Lord (Mark 13:3). And then at the Transfiguration (Matthew 17:1), at the home of Jairus whose daughter was raised from the dead (Mark 5:37), and in the Gethsemane garden (Matthew 26:37), it was only the trio of Peter, James, and John who were invited in. From this inner circle of three we are narrowed down to two, Peter and John. It was these two apostles who were charged by Jesus with the responsibility of making the preparations for the Passover (Luke 22:8). Of these two, Peter's close relationship to Jesus is well documented in Scripture. Which brings us now to the *one*, John. No less than five times in the gospel of John is John singled out as the one whom Jesus loves (John 13:23).

That Jesus loved all His disciples is clear from John 13:1, "Having loved his own who were in the world, he now showed them the full extent of his love." But John does occupy a special place. He had a greater intimacy with Jesus than the other disciples.

The teaching of Scripture is clear. God does not show favoritism (Acts 10:34-35; Ephesians 6:9). God has no favorites, but He does have his intimates. Abraham was called God's friend. Moses was privileged to know God's ways. David was called a man after God's own heart. Daniel was highly esteemed. And what was a common characteristic to be found in all of these men: Abraham, Moses, David, Daniel and John? Without question, they were all men who through prayer sought to know God more intimately.

Do you desire to know God more deeply? Then you know what you must do. Pray when you feel like it. Pray when you don't feel like it. Pray until you do feel like it!

"The prayer of a righteous man can bring powerful results."
James 5:16, The Norlie Translation

Chapter 8

THE SERMON AMERICA MOST
WANTS TO HEAR

A national survey revealed that the 'Sermon America Most Wants to Hear' is about prayer. Specifically, those questioned asked, "How Can I Make Prayer More Effective?"

The Scripture says, "The prayer of a righteous man is powerful and effective" (James 5:16). This is precisely what inquiring spiritual minds want to know. How can I offer prayers that are powerful and effective? That is, prayer that works and prayer that prevails.

People seem interested to know not so much about how prayer works (the mechanics), but about prayer that works (the dynamics). The key, according to James 5:16, is that the prayers should be offered by a righteous person. A righteous person, according to the Bible, is one who has been declared righteous through faith in Jesus Christ. Specifically, a righteous person is one whose life is characterized by the following:

1. A Pure Heart – "If I had cherished sin in my heart, the Lord would not have listened, but God has surely listened and heard my voice in prayer. Praise be to God who has not rejected my prayer ..." (Psalm 66:18-20).

2. Right Motives – "You want something but don't get it. You all covet, but you cannot have what you want. You quarrel and fight; you do not have because you do not ask God. When you ask, you do not receive, because you ask with wrong motives, that you may spend what you get on your pleasures" (James 4:2-3).

3. Obedient Living – "If you remain in me and my words remain in you, ask whatever you wish, and it will be given you" (John 15:7).

4. A Forgiving Spirit – "And when you stand praying, if you hold anything against anyone, forgive him, so that your Father in heaven may forgive you your sins" (Mark 11:25).

5. A Surrendered Will – "This is the confidence we have in approaching God: that, if we ask anything according to his will, he hears us. And if we know that he hears us – whatever we ask – we know that we have what we asked of him" (I John 5:14-15).

6. A Pleasing Life – "Dear friends, if our hearts do not condemn us, we have confidence before God and receive from him anything we ask, because we obey his commands and do what pleases him" (I John 3:21-22).

7. A Recognition of Jesus' Name – "And I will do whatever you ask in my name, so that the Son may bring glory to the Father. You may ask me for anything in my name, and I will do it" (John 14:13-14).

Three examples of such righteous persons praying are:

1. Elijah – So powerful was Elijah's praying that his prayers brought on, as well as ended, a drought that lasted for three-and-a-half years (James 5:17-18) cf. Luke 4:25.

2. Moses – So effective was Moses' praying that his prayers brought to an end fire from the Lord that had fallen in judgment on complaining Israelites (Numbers 11:1-3).

3. Daniel – So effective was Daniel's praying that his prayers shut the mouths of hungry lions that had Daniel on their minds for dinner! (Daniel 6:10-11, 22).

The following story illustrates the power of praying out of a pure heart and with the right motives. Helen Roseveare, a medical missionary in Zaire, Africa, tells us the story in her own words:

"One night I had worked hard to help a mother in the labor ward; but in spite of all we could do she died leaving us with a tiny premature baby and a crying two-year-old daughter. We had difficulty keeping the baby alive, as we had no incubator (with no electricity to run an incubator) and no special feeding facilities. Although we lived on the equator, nights were often chilly with treacherous drafts. One student midwife went for the box we had for such babies and the cotton wool the baby would be wrapped in. Another went to stoke up the fire and fill a hot water bottle. She came back shortly in distress to tell me that in filling the bottle it had burst. Rubber perishes easily in tropical climates. 'And it is our last hot water bottle!' she exclaimed.

As in the west, it is no good crying over spilled milk, so in Central Africa it might be considered no good crying over burst water bottles. They don't grow on trees, and there are no drugstores down forest pathways.

'All right,' I said, 'put the baby as near the fire as you safely can; sleep between the baby and the door to keep it free from drafts. Your job is to keep the baby warm.'

The following noon, as I did most days, I went to have prayers with any of the orphanage children who chose to gather with me. I gave the youngsters various suggestions of things to pray about and told them about the tiny baby. I explained our problem about keeping the baby warm enough, mentioning the hot water bottle. The baby could so easily die if it got chills. I also told them of the two-year-old sister, crying because her mother had died.

During the prayer time, one ten-year-old girl, Ruth, prayed with the usual blunt conciousness of our African children. 'Please, God,' she prayed, 'send us a water bottle. It'll be no good tomorrow, God, as the baby will be dead, so please send it this afternoon.'

While I gasped inwardly at the audacity of the prayer, she added by way of corollary, 'And while You are about it, would You please send a dolly for the little girl so she'll know You really love her?'

As often with children's prayers, I was put on the spot. Could I honestly say 'Amen?' I just did not believe that God could do this. Oh yes, I know that He can do everything. The Bible says so. But there are limits, aren't there? The only way God could answer this particular prayer would be by sending me a parcel from the homeland. I had been in Africa for almost four years at that time, and I had never ever received a parcel from home. Anyway, if anyone did send me a parcel, who would put in a hot water bottle? I lived on the equator!

Halfway through the afternoon, while I was teaching in the nurses' training school, a message was sent that there was a car at my front door. By the time I reached home, the car had gone. But there, on the veranda, was a large twenty-two pound parcel. I felt tears pricking my eyes. I could not open the parcel alone, so I sent for the orphanage children. Together we pulled off the string, carefully undoing each knot. We folded the paper, taking care not to tear it unduly. Excitement was mounting. Some thirty or forty pair of eyes were focused on the large cardboard box. From the top I lifted out brightly colored, knitted jerseys. Eyes sparkled as I gave them out. Then there were the knitted bandages for the leprosy patients, and the children looked a little bored. Next came a box of mixed raisins and sultanas that would make a nice batch of buns for the weekend. Then, as I put my hand in again, I felt the … could it really be? I grasped it and pulled it out: yes, a brand new, rubber hot water bottle!

I cried. I had not asked God to send it. I had not truly believed that He could. Ruth was in the front row of the children. She rushed forward, crying out, 'If God sent the bottle, He must have sent the dolly, too!' Rummaging down to the bottom of the box, she pulled out the beautifully dressed dolly. Her eyes shone. She had never doubted.

Looking up at me, she asked, 'Can I go over with you, Mummy, and give this dolly to that little girl, so she'll know that Jesus really loves her?'

That parcel had been on the way for five whole months; packed up by my former Sunday school class, whose leader had heard and obeyed God's prompting to send a hot water bottle, even to the equator. And one of the girls had put in a dolly for an African child - five months before - in answer to the believing prayer of a ten-year-old to bring it 'that afternoon.' Before they call, I will answer! (Isaiah 65:24)."

America, are you listening?!

Notes

"But if any of you lacks wisdom, let him ask God, who gives to all generously and without reproach, and it will be given to him. But he must ask in faith without any doubting, for the one who doubts is like the surf of the sea, driven and tossed by the wind."
James 1:5-6, New American Standard Bible

Chapter 9

SEVEN KEYS TO ANSWERED PRAYER

The Bible is a long and detailed record of answered prayer. Answered prayer simply means that God grants your request.

For examples of answered prayer we need only to consider the lives of Jacob (Genesis 35:3), Moses, Aaron and Samuel (Psalm 99:6), Hannah (I Samuel 1:20), David (I Samuel 23:4), Zechariah (Luke 1:13), Anna (Luke 2:36-37), Jesus (John 11:41-42) and Paul (Acts 28:8).

Furthermore, the Scripture does, in fact, teach that God answers prayer.

1. "For the eyes of the Lord are on the righteous and his ears are attentive to their prayer" (I Peter 3:12). This is a quotation from Psalm 34:15.
2. "If you believe, you will receive whatever you ask for in prayer" (Matthew 21:22).
3. "This is the confidence we have in approaching God: that if we ask anything according to his will, he hears us. And if we know that he hears us - whatever we ask - we know that we have what we asked of him" (I John 5:14-15).
4. "The Lord is far from the wicked but he hears the prayer of the righteous" (Proverbs 15:29).

Seven Keys to Answered Prayer, although found in just two verses of the Bible, are taught throughout the whole of Scripture. Those two verses are James 1:5 and 6: "If any of you lacks wisdom, he should ask God, who gives to all without finding fault, and it will be given to him. But when he asks, he must believe and not doubt, because he who doubts is like a wave of the sea, blown and tossed by the wind."

Key #1 THERE IS A GENUINE NEED
"If any of you lacks wisdom"

Here James speaks of someone who is lacking in wisdom. This lack is to be understood as a need (cf. Psalm 34:10). "If any of you" leaves it wide open to any believer.

Jesus said, "Ask and it will be given to you; seek and you will find; knock and the door will be opened to you" (Matthew 7:7). Based on Jesus' words, asking implies want, seeking implies loss, and knocking implies need. You ask God because there is something you want. You seek God because there is something you've lost. And you knock at heaven's door because there is something you need. This going to God with a genuine need is beautifully illustrated in the parable of a needy man (Luke 11:5-13).

"Then he said to them, 'Suppose one of you has a friend and he goes to him at midnight and says, 'Friend, lend me three loaves of bread, because a friend of mine on a journey has come to me, and I have nothing to set before him.'"

"Then the one inside answers, 'Don't bother me. The door is already locked, and my children are with me in bed. I can't get up and give you anything.' I tell you, though he will not get up and give him the bread because he is his friend, yet because of the man's boldness he will get up and give him as much as he needs."

"So I say to you: Ask and it will be given to you; seek and you will find; knock and the door will be opened to you. For everyone who asks receives; he who seeks finds; and to him who knocks, the door will be opened."

KEY #2 THERE IS A REQUEST MADE
"He should ask God"

The need is what sends us to God. And in the presence of God the request is made known. This is supported by Paul's teaching in Philippians 4:6: "Do not be anxious about anything, but in everything, by prayer and petition, with thanksgiving, present your requests to God." The point is this. You have to ask!

Of course, it follows that in asking God, you will seek to pray according to His will and not your own (I John 5:14-15).

And furthermore, you will pray in Jesus' name "so that the Son may bring glory to the Father" (John 14:13-14).

KEY #3 THERE IS A RECOGNITION OF THE GOODNESS OF GOD
"Who gives generously to all"

God loves to help. Jesus said, "Which of you, if his son asks for bread, will give him a stone? Or if he asks for a fish, will give him a snake? If you, then, though you are evil, know how to give good gifts to your children, how much more will your Father in heaven give good gifts to those who ask him!" (Matthew 7:9-11).

In keeping with his character, God, who alone is truly good, delights to give to his children. A good God gives good gifts.

KEY #4 THERE IS NO RESENTING BY GOD OF YOUR ASKING
"Without finding fault"

Or as J. B. Phillips puts it: "And if in the process, any of you does not know how to meet any particular problem, he has only to ask God –who gives generously to all men *without making them feel foolish or guilty* – and he may be quite sure that the necessary wisdom will be given him. But he must ask in sincere faith without secret doubts as to whether he really wants God's help or not. The man who trusts God, but with inward reservations, is like a wave of the sea, carried forward by the wind one moment and driven back the next" (James 1:5-6, J.B. Phillips Translation).

The phrase "without finding fault" is translated by the Greek word "oneidizo." Literally it means "to cast in one's teeth." The meaning here is that God will not throw back in your face the request you have made of him. With God there is no reproach, no resenting by him of your asking.

KEY #5 THERE IS THE PROMISE OF PROVISION
"It will be given to him"

You will get God's help. God will not refuse to give you what Jesus died and rose again to obtain for you. "He who did not spare his own Son, but gave him up for us all – how will he not also, along with him, graciously give us all things" (Romans 8:32).

It is the plain teaching of the Bible that what we pray for and receive is what God has already promised to provide. This is clearly illustrated in the story of Hannah, who prayed and asked God for a son (I Samuel 1:11,19,20). Furthermore, we read of God in Numbers 23:19b, "Does he speak and then not act? Does he promise and not fulfill?"

KEY #6 THERE IS THE PRESENCE OF FAITH
"But when he asks, he must believe"

God requires faith on our part. For when we believe (exercise faith in) God, we take him at his word. And this is pleasing to God, because faith is a way of honoring God, of bringing glory to God, by believing that what he says is precisely what he will do.

So very many prayers go unanswered because of a lack of faith. In this regard, read Matthew 13:58, 21:21-22 and Mark 9:14-29. The problem is with our lack of faith, not with God's will or power to answer our prayers. This is illustrated in the story of a man who was covered from head to toe with leprosy and believed that Jesus could heal him. He said, "Lord, *if* you are willing, you can make me clean" (Luke 5:12). He doubted the *willingness* of Jesus to grant him his miracle. Those of us who believe in God believe that God can do all things, but so few of us believe that he will. Faith believes that God *will do* what he promised to do.

KEY #7 THERE IS THE ABSENCE OF DOUBT
"And not doubt, because he who doubts is like a wave of the sea, blown and tossed by the wind"

Doubts arise in the mind. To doubt is to question God, to argue with God. But there is to be no second-guessing, no second thoughts. You may dismiss your doubts as the apostle Thomas did by confessing who Jesus is, "My Lord and my God" (John 20:28).

These seven keys to answered prayer are beautifully illustrated in the following story. Louise Redden, a poorly dressed lady with a look of defeat on her face, walked into a grocery store. She approached the owner of the store in a most humble manner and asked if he would let her charge a few groceries. She softly explained that her husband was very ill and unable to work. They had seven children and they needed food. John Longhouse, the grocer, scoffed at her and requested that she leave his store. Visualizing the family needs, she said: "Please, sir! I will bring you the money just as soon as I can." John told her he could not give her credit, as she did not have a charge account at his store.

Standing beside the counter was a customer who overheard the conversation between the two. The customer walked forward and told the grocer that he would stand good for whatever she needed for her family.

The grocer said in a very reluctant voice, "Do you have a grocery list?" Louise replied, "Yes, sir."

"OK," he said, "put your grocery list on the scales and whatever your grocery list weighs, I will give you that amount in groceries."

Louise hesitated a moment with a bowed head; then she reached into her purse, took out a piece of paper, and scribbled something on it. She then laid the piece of paper on the scale carefully with her head still bowed. The eyes of the grocer and the customer showed amazement when the scales went down.

The grocer, staring at the scales, turned slowly to the customer and said begrudgingly, "I can't believe it."

The customer smiled as the grocer started putting the groceries on the other side of the scales. The scale did not balance, so he continued to put more and more groceries on them until the scales would hold no more. The grocer stood there in utter disgust.

Finally, he grabbed the piece of paper from the scales and looked at it with greater amazement. It was not a grocery list. It was a prayer that said: "Dear Lord, you know my needs and I am leaving this in your hands."

The grocer gave her the groceries that he had gathered and placed on the scales and stood in stunned silence.

Louise thanked him and left the store. The customer handed a fifty-dollar bill to John as he said, "It was worth every penny of it." It was sometime later that John Longhouse discovered the scales were broken. Only God knows how much a prayer weighs!

God has given us the keys to receive affirmative answers to our prayers. God answers true, believing prayer. Go ahead. Ask and you will receive!

Notes

"This sufferer called, and Jehovah heard…"
Psalm 34:6, American Baptist Publication Society

Chapter 10

ANGELS ALL AROUND!

This is a story about angels and answered prayer. It is about angels who came on a rescue mission in answer to prayer. "Are not all angels ministering spirits sent to serve those who will inherit salvation?" (Hebrews 1:14).

While visiting our daughter Charity, a first year law student in Virginia, my wife and I joined her in her compact car to make our way to a local restaurant for an evening out. As we turned into the parking lot, there was a mini-van not too far in front of us that seemed to slow to a stop. Suddenly the side door slid open and out jumped a young boy. The woman driver, unaware that her passenger was exiting, proceeded to move forward to a parking space, only to hear the terrifying scream of the boy who was being dragged under the van. She brought the vehicle to an immediate stop not realizing that the right rear wheel now rested excruciatingly heavy on her grandson's newly sneaker-shod foot. The grandmother had just purchased a new pair of sneakers for her grandson on the happy occasion of his ninth birthday. They were on their way to the restaurant to celebrate.

Our daughter brought her car to a quick stop and we all jumped out with cries to God in heaven for help. I sprinted to the boy's side. My wife rushed to the driver's side. Feverishly I worked with the boy to free his foot from the tons of weight crushing down on it, but to no avail. The grandmother, not knowing exactly what was taking place, moved the vehicle neither forward nor backward, lest something worse happen. It was then that God chose to miraculously intervene on behalf of one of His loved ones.

"This poor man called, and the Lord heard him,
he saved him out of all his troubles.
The angel of the Lord encamps around those
who fear him, and he delivers them" (Psalm 34:6-7).

With the boy screaming in pain for relief, I continued to work with him, struggling to free his trapped foot. And then, miraculously, like a rocket launched from its pad, his foot came flying out of the shoe.

Let's hear the story from another point of view. The boy's grandmother, Ellie Witham, the headmaster of a private school in Chesapeake, Virginia, wrote to me shortly after this incident.

"Dear John,

My grandson, James, was so excited when he received your letter yesterday. He really established a very strong bond with you on that wonderful and awesome evening of the accident.

It was rather strange; I had just told him that there was something wonderful and special about turning nine years old. That in some way we didn't really understand and couldn't explain, life just changed, and in some ways it would never be the same. Little did I know what I was really saying!

I guess James told you that, except for his backsides being scraped and all bruised from being dragged under the van, that he was perfect and whole in every respect. The doctor had to make some adjustments in his back. I guess that, too, happened when he was dragged under the van.

James mentioned several times about all the angels he saw around him that night, and that he saw a really bright white light spinning around the tire that was on top of his feet.

I will always be more than grateful to God for His mercy and grace, His angels and His Presence, for giving my grandson back to me, and whole and perfect, except for the scrapes. I think James still has the imprint of the metal eyelets from the tennis shoes on his feet. Just another reminder to all of us of His goodness, mercy and grace. And every time I look at James, I see and feel God's love all over again.

Thank you so very much for being there, for caring, for stopping and helping us. You were one of God's angels clothed in flesh. Your stopping and helping us with such love, and saying the right things to James, assuring him that he was going to be all right, was a big part of the miracle for all of us that night.

It was just one of those things. I know what happened, I saw what happened, and experienced it with every fiber of my being, and still it is almost beyond my comprehension. And yet I know that I saw what I saw, and lived through all of it. I know that *God truly hears us before we cry.*

Thank you again, and many blessings to you and your loved ones. And my sincere thanks and appreciation to them."

Dear reader, keep your eyes open ... angels are at work! "Isn't it obvious that all angels are sent to help out with those lined up to receive salvation" (Hebrews 1:14, The Message).

"Pray unceasingly."
I Thessalonians 5:17, Greek New Testament

Chapter 11

ALL I CAN DO IS PRAY

How many times in a crisis situation or when a desperate need arises, have you heard someone say, "Well, all I can do is pray." It is spoken as though prayer has been given to us by God only as a last resort. When all else fails, pray. Quite to the contrary. Prayer should be our first resource and not our last resort.

Alfred Lord Tennyson, in "The Passing of Arthur," addresses this lament poetically:

"Pray for my soul.
More things are wrought by prayer
Than this world dreams of.
Wherefore, let thy voice
Rise like a fountain for me night and day.
For what are men better than sheep or goats
That nourish a blind life within the brain,
If, knowing God, they lift not hands of prayer
Both for themselves and those who call them friend?
For so the whole round earth is every way
Bound by gold chains about the feet of God."

Prayer is, in fact, divine power, for there are no limitations in receiving from God the things we need according to His promises. Peter wrote, "His divine power has given us everything we need for life and godliness through our knowledge of him who called us by his own glory and goodness. Through these he has given us his very great and precious promises, so that through them you may participate in the divine nature and escape the corruption in the world caused by evil desires" (II Peter 1:3-4).

For those of us who believe, prayer is like a man who, when caught in a storm, prays and keeps on rowing. We are to pray as though everything depends on God, and it does, while keeping our hands to the oars.

When the English author, Rudyard Kipling, lay dying in a hospital a nurse asked him, "Mr. Kipling, is there anything I can do for you?"

He replied, "Only my Father who is in heaven can help me now."

And this is precisely where prayer comes in. Often prayer is a cry for help in time of need. I am reminded of Jonah who prayed from inside the belly of a great fish. He said, "In my distress I called to the Lord, and he answered me. From the depths of the grave I called for help, and you listened to my cry" (Jonah 2:2).

The next time someone says to you in desperation, "All I can do is pray," you may wish to reply, "That's *precisely* what God would *have* you do ... pray and keep on praying."

Notes

"Jabez cried to the God of Israel, saying,
Oh that you would bless me and enlarge my border,
and that your hand might be with me, and you
would keep me from evil so it might not hurt me!
And God granted his request."
I Chronicles 4:9-10, The Amplified Bible

Chapter 12

THE STORY OF JABEZ

After several chapters of genealogical tables in the book of I Chronicles we come upon just two verses that are hidden away for treasure seekers! As you will see, God wanted this incident recorded for our encouragement in prayer.

It is the story of Jabez. "Jabez was more honorable than his brothers. His mother had named him Jabez, saying, 'I gave birth to him in pain.' Jabez cried out to the God of Israel, 'Oh, that you would bless me and enlarge my territory! Let your hand be with me, and keep me from harm so that I will be free from pain.' And God granted his request" (I Chronicles 4:9-10).

Jabez was the head of a family of the tribe of Judah. But why is Jabez singled out? Why, if you will, this historical footnote? To find the answers to these questions, we need to closely examine what little we know of Jabez.

The name Jabez sounds like the Hebrew word for 'pain.' The Hebrew is 'Ya'bes.' It means "he makes sorrowful" or "he giveth pain." Most likely, his mother gave him the name Jabez because it hurt her to bear him. She said, "I was in much pain when I gave birth to him." Evidently Jabez was also in pain for much of his life. Otherwise, he would not have prayed to be free from pain.

You've heard the old saying, "sticks and stones may break my bones, but names will never hurt me!" But names can and do hurt. Jabez was hurting ... hurting badly. Surely, whatever is our headache or heartbreak, we can readily identify with Jabez.

His mother cried at childbirth. Jabez cried at life. His mother called him one name, but Jabez called *upon* another name! He cried out. He called out to the name of the God of Israel. And so

67

the pain in Jabez's life was not lost to him, not wasted on him, because it sent him to his knees; it drove him to God! There's nothing quite like suffering that will propel you to pray. Pain sent Job there. It sent our Lord there. It sent the Apostle Paul there. And it is meant to send you and me there as well. Pain brings with it a sense of urgency. Urgency to find some relief. Job turned to God for relief. And rather than let the pain destroy his life, Jabez sought the Lord for relief as well.

Now the Bible says, "Jabez was more honorable than his brothers" (vs. 9). He was more respected because by fleeing to the God of all grace and compassion, he was enabled by God to triumph over his difficulties. This is why special attention is given in the Bible to Jabez, because by faith in God he triumphed over his name! By faith he triumphed over his pain. He went beyond coping with his pain (a necessary thing); he triumphed over it.

Like Jabez and many others we, too, come to painful places in our lives. And like Jabez we, too, must pray. We must pray like Jabez prayed. The Bible gives us such a prescription for pain: prayer. "Is anyone of you suffering? He should pray" (James 5:13). That is, let him pray and keep on praying until he finds his relief in God.

What exactly did Jabez pray for? Jabez prayed for five things:

1. **PROSPERITY**. First, Jabez prayed for prosperity. "Oh, that you would bless me."

   In effect, he was saying to God, "Please do good things for me." This is legitimate praying. Who doesn't want his/her life blessed of God? You wouldn't ask God not to bless you, would you?

   Do remember: There are the blessed and the not so blessed! Ask God to bless you! Don't be afraid. Go ahead. Ask God even now to bless you.

2. **PROVISION**. Second, Jabez prayed for provision. "And enlarge my territory." Jabez asked God to give him more

land, to enlarge his borders. What is it that you *need* more of? Like Jabez, go to God and ask him for it.

3. **PRESENCE**. Third, Jabez prayed for presence. "Let your hand be with me." Jabez was reaching out for more than just freedom from pain. He was reaching out for God; not just the absence of pain, but for the presence of God. It is when we have the assurance of the presence of God in our lives that we can face, endure and triumph over all the hardships that life serves up to us.

4. **PROTECTION**. Fourth, Jabez prayed for protection. "And keep me from harm." "Dear God," Jabez was praying, "don't let anyone hurt me." There came a time in Jabez's life when God said, "That's enough." When that happens, it is always God's enough.

5. **PLEASANTNESS**. Fifth, Jabez prayed for pleasantness. "That I will be free from pain." Can anything be more pleasant than to be freed from one's pain? Consider the experience of our Lord in his suffering. The Scripture records, "Let us fix our eyes on Jesus, the author and perfector of our faith, who for the joy (pleasantness) set before him, endured the cross (pain), scorning its shame, and sat down at the right hand of the throne of God. Consider him who endured such opposition from sinful men, so that you will not grow weary and lose heart" (Hebrews 12:2-3).

Beyond the pain and suffering of the cross were the joy and the pleasure of being in the very presence of God. So, too, let us not "grow weary and lose heart." For when you walk with the Lord, the best is yet to be!

And how did all of this turn out in Jabez's life? Were his prayers answered? Did he become better or bitter? The Bible gives us the answer: "And God granted his request." Are these not wonderful words? Just think: God did all that Jabez prayed for. God gave him nothing less than all that he asked for.

On the fast track in Great Britain was a runner by the name of Derek Redmond. In the closing meters of a 400-meter race, Derek Redmond pulled a hamstring and, falling to the track, he cried out in pain. He had entered the race to win, but now he was determined to finish. Bruised but not broken, he managed to get up on his feet and started to limp toward the finish line. His father, Jim, was in the viewing stands. Jumping onto the track, he put his arm of support around his son.

"You don't have to do this," he said to his son.

"Yes, I do," said Derek.

"Then we're going to finish this together," said his father.

To a standing ovation from the cheering crowd, father and son crossed the finish line wrapped in each other's arms. They say that the cheers of the crowd that day were even louder than if Derek had won the gold medal.

Whatever the pain in your life right now, the Father's arms are wrapped securely around you and he is saying, in effect, "We're going to finish this together." Pray then. Pray as Jabez prayed.

Notes

I give myself unto prayer."
Psalm 109:4, The Revised Version

Chapter 13

PRAYER AND TRIUMPH

In the book, *Glory Filled the Land*, G. Campbell Morgan makes this statement: "To teach the church to pray is to teach the church to triumph!" Since our churches will triumph only by this prayer power, it is essential that we teach those committed to our care how to pray. The message of this chapter is simply: *To pray is to triumph.*

A church planter in Arizona wrote, "Unless we understand that this life is war, we won't know what prayer is for." The church of Jesus Christ is engaged in a great spiritual battle. The church is not a peacetime army. We are a church at war. There is conflict on every side. The apostle Paul wrote, "For when we came into Macedonia, this body of ours had no rest, but we were harassed at every turn - conflicts on the outside, fears within" (II Corinthians 7:5). The Bible abounds with military metaphors: put on the full armor of God; endure hardship with us like a good soldier of Christ Jesus; the weapons we fight with are not the weapons of the world; fight the good fight of the faith; I have fought the good fight, and so forth. Today we are the church militant and through the awesome release of divine power through prayer we become the church triumphant.

Dr. Kenneth Kantzer, the Senior Editor of Christianity Today magazine, asked a well-known Korean pastor what he thought was the reason for the accelerated growth of the Christian church in Korea. After a deliberate, thoughtful pause of several minutes, he finally replied, "I think it is because we lived under severe Japanese persecution for so long. We learned to have no hope in ourselves, but only in God. And we learned to pray. We have been a suffering church and, therefore, a praying church. That is what I think explains it."

The oldest book in the Bible is the book of Job. It has a great deal to say about prayer and triumph. As a matter of fact, the book opens with prayer and ends in triumph. In the opening verses of Job we see Job engaged in the worship of God, occupied with prayer. His sons used to take turns holding feasts in their homes and they would invite their three sisters to eat and drink with them. When a period of feasting had run its course, Job would send and have them purified. Early in the morning he would sacrifice a burnt offering for each of them, thinking, "Perhaps my children have sinned and cursed God in their hearts." This was Job's regular custom (Job 1:4-5).

Following this, Job faced the ultimate test of his life. He lost his house, his possessions, his job, his health and his children. All this time Job remained silent before God until he lost his children. Then the Scripture says, "At this, Job got up and tore his robe and shaved his head. Then he fell to the ground in worship and said: 'Naked I came from my mother's womb and naked I will depart. The Lord gave and the Lord has taken away; may the name of the Lord be praised.' In all this, Job did not sin by charging God with wrongdoing'" (Job 1:20-22).

There it is, prayer and triumph. Job's devotion to God in worship, expressed through prayer and sacrifice, gives evidence of a deep and abiding commitment to God.

How was Job after his testing was over? Was he bitter? Did he turn aside from following after the Lord? The epilogue of Job's life reads as follows: "After Job had *prayed* for his friends, the Lord made him prosperous again and gave him twice as much as he had before" (Job 42:10).

To pray is to triumph!

Notes

"In your prayers be unwearied."
Romans 12:12, The Conybeare Translation

Chapter 14

MUCH PRAYER - MUCH BLESSING

"When there is much prayer, there is much blessing.
When there is little prayer, there is little blessing.
When there is no prayer, there is no blessing."

Dee Duke, the pastor of Jefferson Baptist Church in Jefferson, Oregon, has framed his ministry around this guiding principle: "Much Prayer - Much Blessing." Here is his story.

Dee grew up on a dairy farm in Washington State. As a young teen he went off to Western Baptist Bible College to increase his knowledge of the Scriptures. His desire was to return to the farm, but God had other plans for him. After graduation, a group of about twenty believers in Jefferson persuaded him to come and be their pastor. Over the next ten years the church grew from the original twenty to two hundred and remained there. The church had plateaued and so had their pastor. Try as he would, the church didn't grow. Dee was working 80 hours a week at the church. He became so discouraged that he came very near to leaving the ministry.

In 1989 Pastor Duke attended his first four-day pastors' prayer summit. He came back determined to change his priorities and those of his church. He said, "I really wanted my church to grow, but I didn't know how to do it." That year his church prayed for ten days before Easter. He asked for 120 people to pray. Prayer would be offered every hour, 24 hours a day, for ten days. Two persons would be praying every hour. One hundred and thirty-one people signed up to pray. That Easter 600 people attended church and 30 of them committed their lives to Jesus Christ.

Before Easter of 1998 several hundred people signed up to pray. Thirty percent of the people praying were under the age of eighteen. Attendance at their four Easter services totaled 1600 people. And what makes this all the more remarkable is that Jefferson, Oregon is a small farming community with a population of only 1800 people!

At one of those pre-Easter prayer marathons, a ten-year old girl prayed for 44 hours. Pastor Duke related that on one occasion when he was praying with her he was sure that if he opened his eyes he would see Jesus. Later on, it became clear to him that she learned to pray by praying with others. Of those ten years of age and older in his church, 50 percent are regularly engaged in prayer.

Pastor Duke teaches on prayer once a month at his church. He says that motivating people to pray is like boiling water; you've got to keep the heat on because the moment you take the kettle off the heat …

Pastor Duke practices what he preaches. He devotes 20 hours or more a week to private and corporate prayer. He has kept this commitment to prayer over the years while also being a husband and father to eight children!

Some of the other ways in which he promotes praying in his church are:

1. Concerts of Prayer held on the third Friday evening of every month.
2. Concerts of Prayer held jointly with the other churches.
3. Every quarter the church commits itself to 24 hours of prayer and fasting.
4. Jericho Praying - everything is done in sevens: the church prays from 7am to 7pm for seven days. This is done prior to sponsoring a Christian music concert in town. The church people pray as they go marching seven times around the track/field where the concert is to be held. Many people have come to faith in Jesus Christ through these outreaches grounded firmly in prayer.

For the Christians in Jefferson Baptist Church "Much Prayer - Much Blessing" is more than a motto. It's a mandate! In answer to the prayers and labors of many, the congregation at Jefferson Baptist has recently moved into its new sanctuary with seating for 1000 people!

Much prayer – much blessing!

Notes

"Please help us by praying for us.
Then many people will give thanks for
the blessings we receive in
answer to all these prayers."
II Corinthians 1:11, Contemporary English Version

Chapter 15

HONEY, WILL YOU HELP ME UP?

Let me share a humorous story with you about a senior lady, told in her own words:

Last November my phone rang. I said, "Hello."

The voice on the other end said, "Are you 'Anna Jean Smith' who attended the old Glenville School in 1924?"

I replied, "Yes, sir, I am."

Then he said, "Do you remember your grammar school sweetheart who gave you your first kiss?"

I said, "Of course I do. A girl never forgets her first kiss."

He replied, "Well, you're talking to him."

My heart skipped a beat. He told me he had a photograph of our first grade class and wanted to bring it over the next day.

I said, "Wonderful." I was so excited I didn't sleep a wink.

The next afternoon when I heard a car door slam, I ran to the bathroom to spray on a little more perfume, and with trembling hands I opened the door. After sixty-seven years, it was love at first sight. We talked for hours and got reacquainted.

After several dates he fell on his knees and said, "Honey, I have two questions. First, will you marry me?"

I said, "Yes, I'd love to. What's the second question?"

He said, "Will you help me up?"

This amusing story reminds me of what happens when we pray for others. Our prayers help others to get up. The apostle Paul speaks of this in II Corinthians 1:8-11: "We do not want you to be uninformed, brothers, about the hardships we suffered in the province of Asia. We were under great pressure, far beyond our ability to endure, so that we despaired even of life. Indeed, in our hearts we felt the sentence of death. But this happened that we might not rely on ourselves but on God, who raises the dead. He has delivered us from such a deadly peril, and he will deliver us. On him we have set our hope that he will continue to deliver us, as you help us by your prayers. Then many will give thanks on our behalf for the gracious favor granted us in answer to the prayers of many."

When we pray, asking God to lift us up, we should also remember to petition him to lift up others as well.

General William Booth was the founder of the Salvation Army. On one occasion he was invited to speak at a large gathering in Chicago. Due to illness, he had to cancel. The organizers of the event asked that he send along his message and it would be read to the assembly. He complied, sending his message by telegram. When the telegram was opened and read to the congregation it had in it only one word: "OTHERS."

To be sure, this is consistent with the message of Scripture.

1. "Each of you should look not only to your own interests, but also to the interests of *others*" (Philippians 2:4).

2. "Carry each *other's* burdens, and in this way you will fulfill the law of Christ" (Galatians 6:2).

3. "Love your neighbor [*others*] as yourself" (Matthew 19:19).

Here and elsewhere (see Luke 10:29-37) Jesus defines one's neighbor as the one who is in need. One of the ways in which we can all give to others in need is through prayer. Whether we are rich or poor, educated or uneducated, a young Christian or a mature Christian, physically able or physically challenged - we can pray. One of the great privileges of prayer is that we can give to those who have little to give. We can give without expecting anything in return.

There are burdens in this life that are so heavy, so crushing, that they cannot be borne alone. That is why the apostle Paul exhorts us to come alongside others and help to shoulder their load. Praying for others is a way of doing that. In prayer, you bring before the sovereign Lord the name of the person(s) and the need(s).

Prayer for others is commanded throughout the Bible. For example, I Timothy 2:1-3 says, "I urge, then, first of all, that requests, prayers, intercession and thanksgiving be made for everyone - for kings and all those in authority, that we may live peaceful and quiet lives in all godliness and holiness. This is good and pleases God our Savior."

Not only are we commanded to pray for all those who are in authority over us (government officials, law enforcement officers, parents, teachers, etc.), we are also commanded to pray for those who persecute us (Matthew 5:44) and who mistreat us (Luke 6:28). We are to pray for each other so that we may be healed (James 5:16). And furthermore, we are to "be alert and always keep on praying for all the saints" (Ephesians 6:18).

With all this in mind, you might consider some "scheduled" praying along these lines -

Sunday	pray for all the saints
Monday	pray for ministries (including your pastor and church)
Tuesday	pray for the troubled
Wednesday	pray for the weak
Thursday	pray for those who are being tested, tried or tempted
Friday	pray for family and friends
Saturday	pray for the sick and suffering

The Bible teaches that we are actually sinning against God if we do not pray for others. In the prophet Samuel's farewell speech to the nation of Israel, he said, "As for me, far be it from me that I should sin against the Lord by failing to pray for you" (I Samuel 2:23).

Praying for others is one of the great and grand privileges of the Christian life. And it most assuredly brings with it a reward. "God is not unjust; he will not forget your work and the love you have shown him as you have helped his people and continue to help them" (Hebrews 6:10).

How lovely it is to think of how our prayers can race across the heavens and chase across the miles to ask for God's intervention in any situation. For through the incredible power of prayer, there is no distance; there is no one and no thing that is beyond God's reach.

This concluding story illustrates powerfully the wonderful results that can happen when we pray for others.

Edith Burns was a wonderful Christian who lived in San Antonio, Texas. She was the patient of a doctor by the name of Will Phillips. Dr. Phillips was a gentle doctor who saw patients as people. His favorite patient was Edith Burns.

One morning he went to his office with a heavy heart and it was because of Edith Burns. When he walked into that waiting room, there sat Edith with her big black Bible in her lap earnestly talking to a young mother sitting beside her. Edith Burns had a habit of introducing herself in this way: "Hello. My name is Edith Burns. Do you believe in Easter?" Then she would explain the meaning of Easter, and many times people would be saved.

Dr. Phillips walked into that office and there he saw the head nurse, Beverly. Beverly had first met Edith when she was taking her blood pressure.

Edith began by saying, "My name is Edith Burns. Do you believe in Easter?"

Beverly said, "Why, yes I do."

Edith said, "Well, what do you believe about Easter?"

Beverly answered, "Well, it's all about egg hunts, going to church, and dressing up."

Edith kept pressing her about the real meaning of Easter and finally led her to a saving knowledge of Jesus Christ.

Dr. Phillips said, "Beverly, don't call Edith into the office quite yet. I believe there is another delivery taking place in the waiting room."

After being called into the doctor's office, Edith sat down. She took one look at the doctor and said,

"Dr. Will, why are you so sad? Are you reading your Bible? Are you praying?"

Dr. Phillips answered gently, "Edith, I'm the doctor and you're the patient." With a heavy heart he said, "Your lab report came back and it shows you have cancer, and Edith, you're not going to live very long." Edith said, "Why Will Phillips, shame on you. Why are you so sad? Do you think God makes mistakes? You have just told me I'm going to see my precious Lord Jesus, my husband and my friends. You have just told me that I am going to celebrate Easter forever, and here you are having difficulty giving me my ticket!"

Dr. Phillips thought to himself, "What a magnificent woman this Edith Burns is!"

Edith continued coming to Dr. Phillips. Christmas came and the office was closed through January 3rd. On the day the office opened, Edith did not show up. Later that afternoon Edith called Dr. Phillips and said she would have to be moving her *story* to the hospital and added, "Will, I'm very near home, so would you make sure that they put women in here next to me in my room who need to know about Easter?"

They did just that. Women began to come in and share that room with Edith and many were saved. Everyone on that floor, from staff to patients, was so excited about Edith that they started calling her Edith Easter; that is, everyone except Phyllis Cross, the head nurse.

Phyllis made it plain that she wanted nothing to do with Edith because she was a "religious nut." She had been a nurse in an army hospital. She had seen and heard it all. She was the original G. I. Jane. She had been married three times. She was hard, cold, and did everything by the book.

One morning the two nurses who were to attend to Edith were sick. Edith had the flu and Phyllis Cross had to go in and give her a shot. When she walked in, Edith had a big smile on her face.

She said, "Phyllis, God loves you and I love you, and I have been praying for you."

Phyllis Cross said, "Well, you can quit praying for me. It won't work. I'm not interested.

Edith said, "Well, I will pray and I have asked God not to let me go home until you come into the family."

Phyllis Cross replied, "Then you will never die because that will never happen," and curtly walked out of the room.

Every day Phyllis Cross would walk into the room and Edith would say, "God loves you, Phyllis, and I love you, and I'm praying for you." One day Phyllis Cross said she was literally drawn to Edith's room like a magnet would draw iron. She sat down on the bed and Edith said, "I'm so glad you have come, because God told me that today is your special day."

Phyllis Cross said, "Edith, you have asked everybody here the question, 'Do you believe in Easter?' but you have never asked me."

Edith said, "Phyllis, I wanted to ask many times, but God told me to wait until you asked and now you have."

Edith Burns took her Bible and shared with Phyllis Cross the Easter story of the death, burial and resurrection of Jesus Christ.

Edith said, "Phyllis, do you believe in Easter? Do you believe that Jesus Christ is alive and that He wants to live in your heart?"

Phyllis Cross said, "Oh, I want to believe that with all of my heart, and I do want Jesus in my life."

Right there, Phyllis Cross prayed and invited Jesus Christ into her heart. For the first time, Phyllis Cross did not walk out of a hospital room, she was carried out on the wings of angels.

Two days later Phyllis Cross came in and Edith said, "Do you know what day it is?"

Phyllis Cross said, "Why, Edith, it's Good Friday."

Edith said, "Oh, no, for you every day is Easter. Happy Easter, Phyllis!" Two days later, on Easter Sunday, Phyllis Cross came in to work, did some of her duties, then went down to the flower shop and got some Easter lilies. She wanted to see Edith, wish her a Happy Easter, and give her some flowers. When she walked into Edith's room, Edith was in bed, that big black Bible on her lap, and her hands on that Bible. There was such a sweet smile on her face. When Phyllis Cross went to pick up Edith's hand, she realized Edith had died. Her left hand was on John 14. "In my Father's house are many mansions. I go to prepare a place for you, I will come again and receive you to Myself, that where I am, there you may be also." Her right hand was on Revelation 21:4, "And God will wipe away every tear from their eyes, there shall be no more death, nor sorrow, nor crying, and there shall be no more pain, for the former things have passed away."

Phyllis Cross took one look at that dead body and then lifted her face toward heaven and with tears streaming down her cheeks, said, "Happy Easter, Edith – Happy Easter!" Phyllis Cross left Edith's body and walked out of the room and over to a table where two student nurses were sitting. She said, "My name is Phyllis Cross. Do you believe in Easter?"

"A cheerful heart makes a quick recovery,
it is crushed spirits that waste a man's frame."
Proverbs 17:22, The Knox Translation

Chapter 16

PRAYER: THE MEDICINE OF COMFORT

Prayer is good medicine. It brings comfort, it gives hope, it brings healing. The psalmist said, "I love the Lord, for he heard my voice; he heard my cry for mercy. Because he turned his ear to me, I will call on him as long as I live" (Psalm 116:1-2). Is there anything more comforting than knowing that when you pray, pouring out your heart and soul to God, that he actually listens to you and comes to your aid? Here is a God who comforts and encourages by coming alongside us in answer to our prayers.

Proverbs 17:22 says, "A cheerful heart is good medicine, but a crushed spirit dries up the bones." What better way to cheer the heart than prayer. Prayer is a gracious means whereby we can commune in our hearts with God, "finding as he promised, perfect peace and rest."

Prayer also gives you hope. As you pray, your confidence in God will grow, hope will rise. Hope means a confident expectation of better things to come. You begin to believe there is, indeed, an assured outcome of your situation, whatever it might be.

The following story is good medicine, the medicine of hope. It happened in Ft. Payne, Alabama during February 1999. There was a couple whose six-year old boy had a very rare brain tumor. Without treatment it would kill him. They had been told there was only one doctor in the world who had experienced success with that particular type tumor. The problem was that the doctor was in Asia. The family, their friends, and their church all prayed for God's compassion as this little boy grew weaker and weaker. The family could not afford to take the boy to Asia for the necessary surgery. As a matter of fact, they couldn't afford the surgery even if they had access to the doctor.

Consequently, most of the prayers offered were simply to ask God to prevent the child from suffering.

The boy's dad was a salesman at a local Ford dealership. One day a very well-dressed man stopped at the dealership. The father talked to him. He obviously could afford it, but the man explained that he didn't need a vehicle. He added that he wasn't sure why he had even stopped. The father suggested that they go into his office talk and look over some brochures. As they exchanged introductions the father discovered the man had the same last name as the Asian doctor who could operate on his son's tumor. Hearing the name, the father fell to his knees and wept. He began praying that the man might be a relative, perhaps a brother, or that at least this man would know the doctor. He was thinking that if the stranger were a family member or knew the doctor maybe he could intervene and make some arrangements to get help for his son.

Noticing what was happening, the other staff members of the dealership began gathering around the father and the stranger. The man was more than a little surprised by this reaction to his name. It was only when the father related the story about his son's tumor that it all began to fall into place for him.

For, you see, the man was not a family member of the doctor or even someone who knew the doctor. **He was the doctor!** He explained that he was moving from Asia to begin practicing medicine in the United States. In fact, he was going to practice medicine at the University of Alabama Hospital in Birmingham which was just two hours from Ft. Payne. The doctor promised that as soon as he completed his move from Asia to the United States he would perform the surgery on the little boy, free of charge.

Now you might ask: why would a very successful and wealthy doctor from Asia who was in the process of moving his practice to Birmingham, Alabama stop at a Ford dealership in Ft. Payne, Alabama? There is only one answer that makes any sense. God hears our prayers and answers them according to our need. Prayer brings comfort. Prayer gives hope. It is comfort for the comfortless. It is hope for the hopeless.

Prayer is also good medicine because it brings healing. Does God heal through prayer? The answer according to the Bible is yes. In Mathew 8:14-17 we read, "When Jesus came into Peter's house, he saw Peter's mother-in-law lying in bed with a fever. He touched her hand and the fever left her, and she got up and began to wait on him. When evening came, many that were demon-possessed were brought to him, and he drove out the spirits with a word and healed all the sick. This was to fulfill what was spoken through the prophet Isaiah: 'He took up our infirmities and carried our diseases'."

Matthew saw a fulfillment of Isaiah's words in Jesus' healing ministry because ultimately sickness results from sin which Jesus paid for with his life. All the healings that Jesus performed in his earthly ministry were advance blessings of the cross. Since Jesus is the same yesterday, today, and forever (Hebrews 13:8), the blessings continue.

Furthermore, studies from medical science have shown that prayer can have a beneficial effect on high blood pressure, wounds, headaches, and anxiety.

When we pray for others, how reassuring to know that God can heal as well at a mile as at a meter! Distance simply doesn't matter. For a beautiful illustration of this truth read the account of the healing of a centurion's servant in Luke 7:1-10.

There is a biblical prescription for anyone who is sick. In James 5:13-14 the sick person can demonstrate his faith in God for healing by calling on the elders of the church. After anointing the sick person with oil, the elders are to demonstrate their faith by calling on the name of the Lord. The Scripture then declares, "And the prayers offered in faith will make the sick person well; the Lord will raise him up" (James 5:15). Note well: it is not the elders or the anointing oil that makes the sick person well. It is the Lord who answers the prayers of the righteous (James 5:15-16).

The power of prayer, operating through faith to bring the desired healing, is illustrated in the following true story. The fourth of July 1983 was a celebrative holiday for the Andrew

Moore family in southern New Hampshire. Parents Andy and Diane and their children, Alison age 4, and Adam age 2, enjoyed hot dogs and hamburgers grilled over charcoal embers accompanied by fresh strawberries plucked from the garden. These were the ingredients for the perfect picnic.

This slice of Americana, however, turned sour the next day. Alison complained of stomach pains accompanied by diarrhea. After two trips to the doctor's office, Alison was admitted to Nashua Memorial Hospital in Nashua, New Hampshire. Blood tests revealed that she had acquired the E-coli bacteria. The diagnosis was hemolytic uremic syndrome which causes kidneys to go into renal failure. Due to the seriousness of Alison's condition, she was transferred to the Intensive Care Unit of the Children's Hospital in Boston. Her condition was so rare at that time that the hospital was only seeing seven to ten patients a year with that illness.

Fortunately, a renowned nephrologist (kidney specialist), Dr. Warren Grupe, was assigned to Alison. He immediately put her on peritoneal dialysis. For two and a-half weeks in the hospital Alison had not put out a drop of urine. Her doctors were seriously talking about the possibility of a kidney transplant if, indeed, one were available.

Alison's mother Diane who is a registered nurse stayed with her daughter in the hospital throughout this ordeal. One Friday Alison's father Andy had just walked in the door of his house after a visit to the hospital when he was greeted by the unwelcome ringing of the telephone. It was Diane. Alison's condition had worsened. She wasn't responding to any medical treatment. She had gone into a renal crisis. They feared they were losing her. Before returning immediately to the hospital (an hour's drive away) Andy called me, his pastor. Previously, I had shared with Andy and Diane a biblical prescription for divine healing from James 5:13-18. I had asked them to prayerfully consider this option.

Andy and Diane were new in their Christian faith. Although they believed in the Bible and considered themselves to be devout Christians, it was still a big decision for them to make.

They felt that their faith was actually being put to the test. They likened making this decision to signing their names to a $100,000 promissory note.

It should be noted here that during this time a twenty-four hour prayer vigil had been established in the church. Day and night, night and day, families were pleading Alison's case with their prayers to God in heaven.

The decision was made. Andy and Diane asked for me to come with the spiritual leaders of the church to pray over Alison. As Diane remembers that day, everything that could go wrong went wrong. My wife Joanie and I got stuck in Boston traffic. We couldn't find a parking space, etc. When we finally arrived at the hospital, the doctors and nurses kindly consented to withdraw giving us the opportunity to be about our Father's business.

"Jesus loves me this I know
For the Bible tells me so
Little ones to him belong
They are weak but he is strong."

With anointing oil in hand, we offered up prayers of faith. "Oh, sweet Jesus, make Alison well again! Let your name be glorified in the healing of this child." As we prayed over Alison, we felt what seemed like electricity coursing through her body and ours. Within twelve hours Alison was putting out urine! It was a miracle! Our prayers were answered! All the doctors and nurses were talking about it. The word they kept using over and over again was *amazing*. Amazing grace, to be sure!

After Alison's healing Diane approached one of her doctors. She asked him if he believed in God. He somewhat hesitatingly said yes. She then asked him if he believed God had healed Alison. Nodding his head, he replied with a firm yes!

Today Alison is a grown woman 21 years of age. She's spending this summer with some friends in Montana. Her mom told me on the telephone last night that Alison is as healthy as a horse. Fits right in with Montana, doesn't it?

Thank you, God.

"Use every kind of prayer and entreaty, and
at every opportunity pray in the Spirit."
Ephesians 6:18, The Goodspeed Translation

Chapter 17

NEVER MISS AN OPPORTUNITY TO PRAY

After shopping at our local Wal-Mart store I returned home only to discover that my 'Daytimer' was missing. My 'Daytimer' notebook is my daily schedule planner. I can't imagine how I would function without it.

Remembering that I had left the 'Daytimer' in the shopping cart, I immediately returned to the store. No one had turned it in. I prayed, "Dear God, may it please you to have some kind soul return it to me." The day passed. Nothing. The next morning the telephone rang. I answered it. "Hello," I said. The voice on the other end of the line said, "Hello, this is Moses calling." I said, "Oh." I mean, when was the last time Moses called you on the phone?! Moses said, "Are you John Evans?" I replied, "Yes, I am." He said, "Well, I have your daily planner. I found it in a shopping cart at Wal-Mart."

Now you must understand that I am a firm believer that our Lord Jesus can find lost things for us. After all, he finds lost people doesn't he? Since he finds lost people, surely he can find lost things like car keys, a wallet, my Wheaton College graduation ring (lost on a wide expanse of sandy beach in New Hampshire and found by a stranger!), etc. These are just a few of my personal things that the Lord has found for me in answer to prayer.

Now the point I wish to make is this: never miss an opportunity to pray. The Bible says, "In everything, by prayer and petition, with thanksgiving, present your requests to God" (Philippians 4:6). Everything by prayer. This is supported further by Paul's statement in Ephesians 5:20, "Always *giving thanks* to God the Father *for everything*, in the name of our Lord Jesus Christ." Since we are to do everything by prayer, we must be careful never to miss the opportunities the Lord gives us to pray.

The apostle Paul addresses this matter in the "Four Alls of Prayer" in Ephesians 6:18. In context, the different parts of the gospel armor have been described, and now the apostle is saying that each piece must be put on with prayer. Prayer is the greatest spiritual weapon of all in our battle against the forces of darkness. "All," or its equivalent, is used 4 times in this one verse. So, let's put on the "overalls" of prayer.

The Four Alls of Prayer:

1. All Occasions
2. All Kinds of Prayers
3. Always Keep on Praying
4. All the Saints

All Occasions. Literally, this means "in every season." We are not merely to pray when there is some crisis or conflict or on special occasions, but rather we are to pray at every opportunity. We are to pray when it is convenient and when it is not.

When talking on the telephone, if a need is mentioned, ask the person with whom you are speaking if you could take a moment and pray together about it over the phone.

Riding along in the car, over the table in a restaurant, walking in the park, while greeting one another after church, wherever and whenever, without calling undue attention to yourself, pray. Stop right then and there and pray.

When someone asks you to remember something in prayer and you say, "Yes, I will," if feasible, why not pray at that moment so you won't forget? The impression it leaves on you will remind you to take it into the prayer closet.

On my way to the "Stand in the Gap" Promise Keepers' Rally in Washington, D.C., I stopped off in Rehoboth Beach, Delaware. With a free day at my disposal, I rented a bicycle and proceeded to ride along the hardened sand at the ocean's edge. The tide was lapping at my bicycle tires, the sea spray was blowing in my face as I raced along the beach, indulging in every luxurious moment of this exhilarating ride. When I finished, I hoisted my bicycle onto the boardwalk for the return trip. A voice, seemingly coming out of nowhere, spoke to me and said,

"I've never seen anyone ride along the beach before." As I turned around I saw a woman standing there. Sensing that this was one of those "divine appointments," I struck up a conversation with her. Rather than getting back into the saddle of my bike I walked along with her. After we introduced ourselves and had a brief exchange of pleasantries, she proceeded to open her heart to me. She had come to this resort town from Ohio as she did every autumn. This time, however, was different. She had come mourning and with two good reasons: her husband had died and her son was living a rebellious life. She strongly suspected that her son was doing drugs. At this point we were running out of both boardwalk and time. We were soon to part company. As we stood there knowing we would probably never meet again I asked, "Would you allow me to pray for you and your son?"

With a mother's heart breaking for her son she said, "Would you?" Off to one side of the boardwalk with babies in strollers passing by, young lovers pedaling by on tandem bikes, and other passers-by looking on, I prayed for her. The sun didn't stand still. The ocean waves continued to clean the face of the sand. All the while heaven was listening. God is always attentive to our prayers. Hearts melted ... burdens were lifted ... God was glorified! Never miss an opportunity to pray.

Surely, God works in strange and mysterious ways. He brought a woman from Ohio and a man from Arizona to the State of Delaware. For what? For the purpose of prayer. Truly, God is amazing.

All Kinds of Prayers. We are to pray "with all kinds of prayers and requests." The word for "prayers" is the general word for prayer. It means to always be in the attitude of prayer. "Requests" are to be understood as "continued strong and incessant pleadings until the prayer is answered."

One day I was visiting a little boy in the hospital. On the way down the corridor I was surprised to see a pastor friend being wheeled to a room prepared for him. He looked terrible. As I spoke with him his wife just stood in the background shaking her head as if to indicate there was not much hope for him. I accompanied him to his room and his wife left us alone. He broke down crying and said, "I'm dying." I then learned that he had had heart surgery. He had been released from the hospital and appeared to be doing well, but infection set in. Now a second surgery was being considered.

I asked if I might read the 90th Psalm to him. At verse ten I read, "The length of our days is seventy years or eighty, if we have the strength; yet their span is but trouble and sorrow, for they quickly pass, and we fly away."

I asked him, "Clay, how old are you?"

He said, "Seventy-one."

I asked, "Do you want to live?"

He said, "Yes."

Then I said, "Would you agree with me that we ask God to increase your strength and extend the years of your life?"

He said, "Yes."

We prayed. God said, "Yes."

Two days later Clay left the hospital. Today he is ministering the Word of God in a mobile home park for seniors in a neighboring town. Never miss an opportunity to pray!

Always Keep on Praying. Literally, this means "watching with all *perseverance*." It means to be awake or alert. We are never to give up except to the will of God.

All the Saints. We are to pray for Christians everywhere. Most especially, we should pray for those who are being persecuted for the sake of the gospel.

In the very next verse (Ephesians 6:19), Paul requests prayer for himself. "Pray also for me." His request is not for his comfort or his peace or even his freedom from prison, but for his testimony to Jesus Christ.

This epistle ends as it began (Ephesians 1:16 ff), with prayer. Paul practiced what he preached. Never miss an opportunity to pray!

Notes

"When I am in trouble, I call to Yahweh,
and he answers me."
Psalm 120:1, The Jerusalem Bible

Chapter 18

KWRB

The phone rang. Crisis? Opportunity? Another sales pitch from a long-distance phone company? No, it was Brayton "Cabby" Back, station manager for our "fledgling" local Christian radio station, *KWRB* (affiliated with HCJB, World Radio Network), or as Cabby puts it "**K**ept **W**ith **R**ighteous **B**lessings." I write "fledgling" because, quite frankly, at the time of his phone call there was no station to manage. Yes, this is another of those miracle-working wonders of God to call into existence something that was not in answer to the prayers of his people.

To back up for just a moment, Cabby, now retired from the Coast Guard, had sold his house in Texas and moved bag and baggage with his wife Sherry to our southeastern Arizona town. Their purpose in coming here was to raise sufficient support for the radio station and to get it on the air broadcasting 24 hours a day, seven days a week.

Back to the phone. Cabby's waiting.

"Hello."

"Hi John, this is Cabby."

"Hi Cabby, how are you?"

"That's what I'd like to talk to you about. May I come over?"

"Sure, when would you like to come?"

"I'll be right over."

I welcomed Cabby at my home. His face revealing the strain, he began to speak. "John, we've been here for nine months now, as you know. Our original goal was to raise the $50,000 necessary to purchase the radio equipment and go on the air. We have since reduced our goal to $20,000 to acquire the minimum amount needed to begin broadcasting. Basically, it will be a "suitcase" operation. With 20 days to go before our deadline, we have $3,889.24. A long, long way from our goal."

"The good news is that God has provided a studio location in answer to all of our prayers. (Note: Cabby is a part of our "Praying Pastors" and ministry leaders who meet every week to pray over our ministries and our community.) We found an office to rent with 1200 square feet for $500 a month and in a great downtown location. And God has provided the rent money for the first year underwritten by some local churches and businesses. John, we praise God for this. But now I'm at a loss to understand where we go from here. If we don't raise the additional sixteen thousand dollars in the next three weeks our Federal Communications Commission license will expire, and we'll have to move back to Texas. John, what do you think we should do?"

"Cabby," I replied, "let's get down on our knees right here by the couch and ask God for wisdom to know how to proceed. Surely, God has the answer."

After a period of prayer, I suggested to Cabby that he gather together all the people he knew in our town who were really supportive of this radio ministry. We would meet to pray and ask God to supply the remaining funds. We set the meeting for the following Tuesday at 7:00 p.m. The word was passed, invitations given, and with hopeful hearts we continued to pray towards the upcoming prayer meeting.

Personally, I was expecting about fifty people to attend. To our dismay, only fourteen people showed up. The look of disappointment on Sherry's face was monumental. The tears would come later.

I asked Cabby to share the need. I then suggested that we press on in prayer and ask God to meet this need. We went around the circle, one after the other, and we prayed. We prayed for one hour. Some in our small group were too overcome with emotion to pray out loud. But pray we did. Then we went home, leaving it all in the hands of God.

About a week later I was in New England for a meeting. The phone rang early one morning in the house of some friends, Don

102

and Darlyne Entrekin, where I was staying as a guest. I was called to the phone. Cabby and Sherry Back were on the line.

"John, we have good news! God has answered our prayers and in a way we never expected. An organization that we didn't even know existed has designated funds for KWRB to get it up and running! We praise God, John. We praise God. And we wanted you to be the first to know."

As I listened, standing there some 2,700 miles away, Cabby and Sherry's words crackled with intense joy.

In the KWRB radio newsletter Sherry shared a quote that she had written in her Bible. A dear friend had passed it on to her. "God's method of supplying help is at the eleventh hour. He always waits until the last minute to reveal His answer. If He didn't, we could not learn faith." That same newsletter carried this caption as well: "Faith makes things possible – not easy!"

Cabby reminded Sherry that they had been in Arizona for nine months, the same amount of time it takes to carry a baby. Sherry's reply: "I think having a baby is easier!"

KWRB is broadcasting 24 hours a day now, seven days a week. There is not a minute when God's voice is not being heard in our county. "The heavens declare the glory of God; the skies proclaim the work of his hands. Day after day they pour forth speech; night after night they display knowledge. There is no speech or language where their voice is not heard. Their voice goes out into all the earth, their words to the ends of the world" (Psalm 19:1-4).

There is a personal postscript to this story. Our son Jeremy, who was just recently graduated from high school, had a radio show on KWRB. Together with a college student, they played contemporary Christian music and offered commentary to teens on a show called "Saturday Afternoon Live." That was something that we had not envisioned. How good of God to provide such on-the-job training and ministry opportunity for some youth in our Christian community.

By the way, Jeremy and his co-host, Josh, refer to the call letters of KWRB as standing for "**K**ickin' It **W**ith the **R**ighteous **B**rothers!" Right on!

**"I love the Lord because he hears
my prayers and answers them."
Psalm 116:1, The Living Bible**

Chapter 19

PRAY AND OBEY

One of the petitions in the Lord's prayer is, "Your will be done on earth as it is in heaven" (Matthew 6:10). Disciples of Jesus Christ are to pray that just as God's will is carried out in heaven so may it be carried out on earth. God's will is to be obeyed. We are to pray and obey. God reveals His will to us in the Bible. He reveals it not so that we might consider it, but so that we might do it. God's will is for doing!

I read of a Korean student who visited his alma mater, Princeton Theological Seminary, several years ago and confessed to one of his professors, "Dr. Moffatt, I'm not a very good preacher, but my church now has 15,000 members."

Recently, he visited again and said, "Dr. Moffatt, I'm still not a good preacher, but my church now has 30,000 members." He might not have been a good preacher, but it was disclosed that his prayer life was exceptional! Here was a man who learned a simple but rewarding lesson: Pray and obey.

One of the most compelling stories I've read that illustrates the power behind *Pray and Obey* comes from the life of Helen Turner of Augusta, Georgia. Her story was published in the 1997 March issue of *Life Magazine* under the heading of, "The Power of Prayer: How Americans Talk to God." Here is Helen's story in her own words:

"In 1968 I went to jail for assault, battery and attempted murder, and the Lord worked a miracle on me. I was waiting to be sent to where I was going to do my time. In my mind I saw her, my husband's mistress, sleeping in my bed, wearing my clothes. And I thought now what good did it do to me to do all this? And I remembered the Scripture and how the Lord set Paul and Silas free from jail. I said, "Lord, if you get me out of here, I'll live for you the rest of my life." That day I began to read my Bible and fast and pray. On the third day the matron said, "Keep doing whatever you're doing, because you're free to go home." My third husband and I held Bible study at our house. Soon, so many people were coming we went to my sister's house, which was a crack house. People wanted to be saved. We packed that house. Prayer changes things. They come to me now and let me know that they're not in "the cut" anymore. But there are new ones, seven-year olds out there selling crack. People call me day and night: "Ma'am, I need you to pray for me. I'm sick of being on all these rocks." All they want is instant relief, but I pray for them. I promised God. That's why I go to the jail, too. Some of them get what you call Jailhouse Salvation. But there's some that mean business. People won't read the Bible, but they'll read me. People look at me, and they're amazed. I was a nobody. My mama had to sell scrap iron for a living. When I was 12, my first husband had to send me to school like he was my daddy. People said I would never amount to more than a fifty-cent whore. Now they say, "I remember what you used to do." I say, "I've done things you don't even know. And I'm still not what I want to be. But I can sure thank God I'm not what I used to be."

Now, 30 years later, Helen is serving as the pastor of the Temple of Prayer and Deliverance Undenominational Church in Augusta. She prayed and she obeyed. She kept her promise to God.

Notes

"Evening, morning, and at noon, I nurse
my woes and groan. He has heard my cry."
Psalm 55:17, A Rendering of the Book of Psalms

Chapter 20

PRAY NOT PREY

The year was 605 B.C. Daniel was a teen-age Jewish boy who had been captured and taken into exile to Babylon. It is now some 67 years later and Daniel is in his eighties.

As an administrator Daniel looked after the king's interests especially with regard to revenue. He proved himself so able in his work that his fellow workers couldn't find a thing to criticize about Daniel or his work. So whether out of personal jealousy or racial prejudice or both, they said in effect, "Our only chance is his religion."

His adversaries seized upon a plan whereby they persuaded the king to issue an edict that "anyone who prays to any god or man during the next thirty days, except to you, O king, shall be thrown into the lions den" (Daniel 6:7). This law, commonly referred to as *the law of the Medes and Persians,* was one that could not be changed or cancelled.

Needless to say, this was a testing of Daniel's faith. If he obeyed the law, he would not be able to pray directly to God. If he disobeyed it, he would appear to be disloyal to the king.

Daniel's habit of prayer reveals his unbroken devotion to God. "Now when Daniel learned that the decree had been published, he went home to his upstairs room where the windows opened toward Jerusalem. Three times a day he got down on his knees and prayed, giving thanks to his God, just as he had done before" (Daniel 6:10). No panic here. No change in plan. Daniel did what he always did everyday. He prayed. Three times a day he prayed.

And what might Daniel have prayed? A prayer known to Daniel and appropriate to the occasion would have been Psalm 59:1-4:

"Deliver me from my enemies, O God;
Protect me from those who rise up against me.
Deliver me from evildoers and save me from blood-thirsty men.
See how they lie in wait for me!
Fierce men conspire against me for no offense or sin of mine, O Lord.
I have done no wrong, yet they are ready to attack me.
Arise to help me; look on my plight!"

Then, too, following again the lead of David, "But I call to God, and the Lord saves me. Evening, morning and noon I cry out in distress, and he hears my voice" (Psalm 55:16-17). Spiritual victories are not won in the open avenue of life but in the secret places, in the closets of prayer.

The king spent the rest of the day trying to think of some way to rescue Daniel out of this predicament, but he was not successful. And so Daniel was thrown into the lion's den. Tested to the very end of his life, Daniel's faith proved to be genuine.

At dawn's early light, the king rushed to the lion's den. He cried out, "Daniel, servant of the living God, has your God, whom you serve continually, been able to rescue you from the lions?" Daniel answered, "O king, live forever! My God sent his angel, and he shut the mouths of the lions. They have not hurt me, because I was found innocent in his sight. Nor have I done any wrong before you, O king" (Daniel 6:20-22).

Dr. Will Bruce commenting on this wrote, "Daniel was not kept out of the lion's den; he was kept in it!" The lesson here is clear: When in perilous places, pray! Pray so that you will not become prey to the lions! Lions like those of laziness, lust, or loneliness.

Since Daniel was no stranger to God in prayer all the years of his life, he could come now in confidence before the throne of God to receive mercy and find grace to help him in his time of need (Hebrews 4:16).

There is no doubt Daniel wanted God's best for his life. This reminds me of a Sears advertisement. Under three different pictures of a washing machine it was written: GOOD, BETTER, and BEST. What was the difference? To get the best machine you had to pay a higher price.

Like Daniel, unbroken devotion to God, expressed by your prayer life, will demand that you pay a greater price. The price may be great, but the rewards will be greater.

"Another truth. If any two of you on earth
agree in making any prayer ..."
Matthew 18:19, The Four Gospels

Chapter 21

THE POWER OF AGREEMENT

Jesus said that if two believers on earth agree upon any matter for which they are praying, they will receive it from God. "Again I tell you that if *two of you* on earth agree about anything you ask for, it will be done for you by my Father in heaven. For where two or three come together in my name, there am I with them" (Matthew 18:19-20).

For agreement in prayer, the minimum requirement is two. Of course, you can have three or more (v. 20), but the irreducible minimum is two. The word for agree in Matthew 18:19 is the Greek word, sumphoneo. It sounds like our English word for symphony. Literally it means, "in sound together," i.e., harmony! When two or more persons are praying together in keeping with the will of God they are, in fact, praying in harmony.

To illustrate this, I've recounted a true story of several ladies in a neighboring town who came together in what I call *agreeable prayer* and the results that followed.

In a very small mining town in southeastern Arizona, three ladies in an even smaller church began to pray. They said, "Lord, we're just a few old ladies and if this church is to survive, we're going to need some children." They prayed and the Lord sent them over a dozen children. Next they said, "Now, Lord, we're going to need a man to lead us." In answer to their prayers, a layman came from South Carolina to lead them. As he began to visit the people, the church began to grow.

Next they said, "Now, Lord, we have this little room as a meeting place for our church, but it's not even decent." So they prayed, and someone who heard of the need sent $10,000 in starter money. Then they conducted a letter writing campaign and more than $25,000 came in. They now have a beautiful sanctuary that seats about 100 people.

Next they said, "Now, Lord, we're going to need a school to provide for these children you've sent us." So they prayed for a school. The congregation, stepping out in faith, made pledges of one-half the amount needed. After thousands of more dollars had been raised there was still a debt of $5,000 over the school.

At this time the Lord showed the pastor of the church, Rev. Richard Roos, what Nehemiah did in a similar situation. Nehemiah prayed to the Lord for what was needed. Then Nehemiah was directed to approach people who had the means to help him. But Pastor Roos protested to the Lord saying, "I don't like to ask anybody for anything." All the while the burden to do this just got heavier.

The $5,000 debt on the school was now overdue and interest charges began to accrue. As the pastor continued to pray, he said, "Oh, Lord, how long do we have to wait?" After praying with his wife about this need, he went to visit a friend who attended his church. He shared the need and that they were $5,000 short. Pastor Roos then said, "I'm just laying the need out before you, but I'm not asking you for anything." His friend replied, "How much did you say was needed?" The pastor replied, "$5,000." The man responded, "Oh, Okay, I'll bring you a check this Saturday."

Oh, the power that is unleashed, the provisions that are given, the prayers that are answered, when Christians come together in agreeable prayer!

In Matthew 18:19-20, since Jesus makes reference to himself and to the Father in this matter of agreeable praying, it would be wise to ask ourselves these three questions in regard to our requests:

1. Will it bring glory to the Father? (John 14:13)
2. Would Jesus want his name associated with it? (John 14:14)
3. Will it please the Holy Spirit or grieve the Holy Spirit? (John 16:14)

When such prayer is offered in the biblically prescribed manner the Father goes into action (Matthew 18:19). Do take note, however, that the answer is not always immediate. We have the assurance that it will be done, but only and always according to God's timetable.

This coming together to pray is a prayer gathering. To "come together" (Matthew 18:20) (Greek, sunago) means to assemble or to gather together. The noun form means place of assembly, synagogue or congregation. Individual prayer gives way to corporate prayer. The two persons praying could be husband and wife, or brother and sister, or parent and child, or two friends. The three persons praying could be father, mother and child, or three believers.

Again, to illustrate the power of agreement in prayer, Pastor Roos shared this story with me.

In a small Arizona town some ladies of the same congregation were convinced they should pray several times a week that fourteen unbelieving spouses of members of their congregation would accept Jesus Christ as their personal Savior and Lord. For several months they continued praying, and what do you suppose happened? NOTHING AT ALL! But instead of becoming discouraged, these sisters kept right on praying. After eight months, three of those spouses were baptized. A year after they had begun their intercessions, 13 of the 14 had accepted Jesus and had been baptized. However, the 14th person seemed a hopeless case. This man left his wife and traveled to a distant city. In the motel room what should he find but a Bible (doubtless a Gideon's Bible). He did not believe in God, hence he'd never read The Book. But that night, the first one away from home, he felt lonely and strangely yet strongly attracted to that sacred volume, so much so that he actually picked it up, opened it at random and began reading. "A certain man had two sons, and the younger of them said to his father, 'Father, give me the portion of goods that falls to me, (etc.) ... and he journeyed to a far country and there wasted his possessions in prodigal living ..." While reading he began to cry. Picking up the phone, he called his wife's pastor, explaining that he would like to be baptized. That same night he returned home and made peace with his wife and a month later was baptized. At the time of this man's baptism that group of ladies had been praying for 14 months for those 14 unbelieving spouses. Imagine the joy of those 14 spouses and of their life's companions!

But what joy could compare with that of the ladies who had extended themselves every week to pray and pray again, when everything appeared so hopeless. Would you like to taste a bit of their joy? You may!

As we pray, what is it that makes all of this work? It is the Person of Jesus Christ. Jesus said, "For where two or three come together in my name, there am I with them" (Matthew 18:20). Jesus is the one in the middle. He is present by his Spirit in the life of his people.

I am reminded of the story of a physician, Dr. Larry Dossey. A patient of his was dying. The day before the patient's death Dr. Dossey sat at his bedside with his wife and children. The dying man knew he had little time, and he chose his words carefully, speaking in a hoarse whisper. Although he was not a religious person, he revealed that he had recently begun to pray.

"What do you pray *for*?" Dr. Dossey asked.

"It isn't *for* anything," he replied thoughtfully. "It simply reminds me that I am not alone."

The certainty that our prayers will be answered is dependent upon the presence of Christ in our midst. When we pray, we are never alone.

Notes

"And I sought for a man among them, that should make up the hedge, and stand in the gap before me for the land ..."
Ezekiel 22:30, King James Version

Chapter 22

GAP STANDERS

I closed the motel door behind me. Leaning against it, I called out a short, desperate prayer that went something like this. "Oh God! I have nowhere else to turn except to you. So Lord, please, please – meet me in this place."

I had come alone to Portland, Oregon to attend a conference sponsored by Christianity Today and Northwest Renewal Ministries because I had reached a kind of plateau in my life and ministry. I needed to hear from God.

As the week was coming to a close, I went to a workshop on prayer. A pastor was speaking about his own experience. After serving in his church for ten years he, too, had come to a point of desperation in his life. His church had grown from 20 people to 200 and plateaued (see Chapter 14). Then he went to a pastors' prayer summit and returned home with a holy resolve to put prayer first in his life. As I listened to him speak, God began to get hold of my heart. I had always been a praying pastor, but now I knew that God was calling me to a deeper devotion to prayer.

Upon returning to Arizona I shared the fire that was burning in my heart with other pastors. As a result, Pastors Joseph Tumpkin, Chuck Carlson, Randy Youngblood, and I began meeting at one p.m. every week to pray for one hour. We also met during the month for extended times of prayer that lasted up to three hours. Today, seven years later, many pastors and ministry leaders are praying together with us. We are Asian and African-American, Anglo and Latino, Presbyterian and Pentecostal. Some of us baptize by sprinkling and others by immersion, but whatever our differences, we are what heaven is going to look like!

Our fellowship of praying pastors and ministry leaders is called "Gathering Arizona in Prayer" (GAP). There is true biblical support for who we are. In Ezekiel 22:30 we read, "I looked for a man among them who would build up the wall and stand before me in the *gap* on behalf of the land..." In battle, when a wall was breached by the advancing troop, the assignment of greatest danger was the task of repairing the gap. We are to be "GAP STANDERS," standing in the gap before God on behalf of others.

- Abraham was a gap stander   (Genesis 18:16-33)
- Moses was a gap stander   (Exodus 32:1-14)
- Phineas was a gap stander   (Numbers 25:1-13,
      cf. Psalm106:28-1)
- Jesus was a gap stander   (Luke 22:31-32,
      John 17:9-15, Romans 8:34)
- Paul was a gap stander   (Philippians 1:3-5;
      Colossians 1:9)

God's call for intercessors is no different today than it was in ancient times. God is looking for men, women, and children who are willing to risk all, surrender all, and give all to be a gap stander! Ultimately, of course, only Jesus Christ can stand in the gap between God and man. "For there is one God and one mediator between God and men, the man Christ Jesus" (I Timothy 2:5).

Our original group of four pastors who began praying together have prayed together every single week for seven years without exception, unless providentially hindered. Some of the benefits that we have received by committing ourselves to pray together on a weekly basis are:

1. We have found a *SAFE PLACE* where we can confess our faults to one another and pray for one another so that we can be helped and healed. Two of our pastors, Rev. Jim Matthias of Covenant Church and Dr. Joseph Tumpkin of Shiloh Christian Ministries, have been especially used of God in praying for the sick in our meetings.
2. We have found a *SECURE RETREAT* where we are spiritually refreshed by listening to uplifting testi-

monies, participating in spirited singing, and engaging in fervent prayer.

3. We have found a **SPIRITUAL HOME** where we are loved, accepted, valued, and affirmed because we all recognize that we have been washed in the same loving blood of the Savior.

Twice a year our congregations come together in "Prayer Gatherings" to worship and to pray. In doing so, we are demonstrating the unity of the body of Christ in our community. We are giving witness to the truth that, "There is one body and one Spirit … one Lord, one faith, one baptism, one God and Father of all, who is over all and through all and in all" (Ephesians 1:4-6).

Following a recent "Prayer Gathering," one of our pastors, Rev. Brent Nicola of Tree of Life Fellowship, shared these observations. "It was a phenomenal move of God. Our folks are still talking about it. Word's out. I believe God is moving in this thing. We must join Him."

We pastors have drafted the following Mission Statement. "We gather together to ask the Lord's blessing so that we, the Church of Jesus Christ in Cochise County, might be fully awake and living for Jesus." In a word … revival! If revival is to come, we must preach prayer, practice prayer, and be compelled to do it. There is no substitute for persistent, prevailing prayer.

As we prayed, the Holy Spirit directed us to "export" the Pastors' Prayer movement to neighboring towns in our county and elsewhere in order to encourage other pastors. We have prayed with other pastors on the dusty walkways of Tombstone, the roads and country lanes of Cochise County, the fields and farms of New Mexico, and other highways and byways too numerous to mention.

We have prayed in dimly lit, cold church basements, on steel-hard chairs for three hours at a stretch, and on soft, upholstered chairs at the Rio Rico Resort where they turn down your bed at night and put chocolate chip cookies on your pillow.

We have prayed for revival from Huachucha City to Willcox, from Bisbee to Benson, from Mexico to New Mexico.

We have prayed standing up, sitting down, lying down ... and sometimes all night. This is a magnificent thing that God is doing because when you touch the life of a pastor you touch the whole congregation.

One example of the love and unity that God has forged among our pastors can be found in a notice in the entryway of one of our churches. Written by Pastor Jim Fogarty it reads, "It was great having you visit! If you are not sensing Celebration Chapel is where God would place you in His body, try one of these..." The notice lists other churches in the community and ends with the words, "I pray weekly with these brothers. They love the Lord God. They love the body of Christ (you). They desire to do His will and build His kingdom...not their own!" As a result of this devotion to prayer, all of our churches are experiencing significant spiritual and numerical growth.

In our prayer movement the emphasis is on prayer, but the focus is on Jesus Christ. As one contemporary version of Colossians 3:1-2 says, "Don't shuffle along, eyes to the ground, absorbed with the things right in front of you. Look up and be alert to what is going on around Christ. That's where the action is." If through prayer we set our hearts on things above where Christ is, we will receive a fresh and deeper experience of God's power in our lives – and we will triumph!

There's a rumbling in our southwestern desert – and it's not an earthquake! It's the rumbling of REVIVAL. The church in Arizona is waking up to Jesus. We are the church militant – waging war for the souls of men, women, and children. We are the church triumphant – overcoming every foe by the blood of the Lamb and by the word of our testimony!

Notes

**"Wilt not thou thyself again give us life,
that thy people may rejoice in thee."
Psalm 85:6, The Emphasized Bible**

Chapter 23

RUMBLINGS OF REVIVAL

Dr. J. Edwin Orr, a scholar and perhaps this century's foremost historian on religious revivals, came to this conclusion after a lifetime of study (all his study was reduced to this one sentence), "Whenever God is getting ready to do something new, He sets his people to praying."

His study of the Revival of 1857-1859 in the United States bears this out. In 1857, only six people out of a population of 1,000,000 in New York City came together to pray for revival. The second week, 14 came...the third week, 23. Soon all the churches in New York City were filled. Revival broke out. Ten thousand people a week were being converted in New York City alone!

The revival went up the Hudson River and down the Mohawk. For example, the Baptists had so many people to baptize that they couldn't get them into their churches. They had to call on pastors from other churches to help with all the baptisms. They went down to the river, cut a big square hole in the ice, and baptized the new believers in the frigid waters. Now, when Baptists do that, you know they really are on fire!

It would appear that God is moving once again in the hearts of New Yorkers. Rev. David Wilkerson, the founder of Teen Challenge and now serving as the pastor of Times Square Church in New York City, offered these observations in his newsletter.

"Dearly Beloved:
GREETINGS IN THE NAME OF CHRIST OUR LORD!
I hear of Christians across the nation praying for revival. And right now, a mighty spiritual explosion is happening here in New York City – right on Broadway.

TIMES SQUARE CHURCH IS EXPERIENCING A GLO-RIOUS VISITATION OF THE HOLY SPIRIT – EXPRESSED BY AWESOME MANIFESTATIONS OF THE PRESENCE OF JESUS IN OUR MIDST. AND IT IS GROWING IN INTEN-SITY EVERY WEEK.

It is standing room only for Jesus on Broadway. People come hours early and hate to be dismissed. We anticipate such an outpouring of God's Spirit; we hope to be having services every night of the week and eventually services lasting all night long. People cannot find seats, even in our Tuesday night prayer and praise meetings. In my lifetime, I have never witnessed such hunger for God and such yearning to be in the presence of the Lord. On occasion I have had to say to the congregation, "Please go home – it's getting late."

Even now we are having all night prayer meetings. Only intense prayer will bring down the satanic strongholds ruling New York City. Not concerts, not "star" evangelists, not gim-micks – just prayer and repentance.

The Lord's presence has been manifested in every single meeting since we began. IT HAS BEEN SIX YEARS OF CONTIN-UOUS REVIVAL WITH SOULS SAVED IN ALL MEETINGS.

PRAYER HAS BEEN THE KEY TO ALL GOD HAS DONE! **We have no business meetings, no surveys, no studies – everybody prays! We pastors pray – the staff prays – the young and old pray – even the children have wonderful prayer sessions. And God has been answering – yes, *over-answering* our prayers."**

My studies across the years have led me to this same conclu-sion. The key to revival is to seek God, to seek his face in prayer and repentance. Prayer is the key to all God has done in the past. There has never been a revival without heart-searching, self-judging, fervent prayer. Prayer is the key to all that God is doing in the present. And prayer is the key to all that God will be doing in the future. John Wesley wrote, "Everything God does, He does by prayer. God rules the world by the prayers of His saints!"

Evan Roberts, the leader of the Welsh Revival of 1904-1905, put it another way. He said that getting things right with God is the cornerstone of revival. And this, of course, can be accomplished in the prayer closet as you meet your Savior at Calvary, where judgment is met. If we believe that this is true, then we must ask ourselves this question. What would God have me to do as a Christian to get right with Him? Not right in terms of my salvation for that is a finished work, but right in terms of my fellowship with Him.

Here is the application. Plan to have an extended, uninterrupted quiet time in the presence of the Lord. Take your Bible, a notebook, and pen into your meeting place with God. After a period of worshipping the Lord just for who He is, ask this question of the Lord and wait for His answer. "O Lord, what would you have me to do as a Christian to get right with you?" Refer to Psalm 139:23-24, one of the most effective heart-searching prayers that can be found. As you wait upon the Lord, searching the Scriptures, and searching your own heart, write down whatever understanding comes to your mind. Don't worry about organizing your thoughts. You can do that later. Simply record what you understand the Lord to be impressing upon your heart and mind.

Don't be discouraged if answers don't readily come. As needed, keep going to the Lord day-after-day in prayer, seeking an answer to your question. The Lord will answer you in your hour of need. What you are asking God for, in effect, is for Him to do a greater work in your life by the power of his Spirit. When that happens, you will experience times of refreshing from the presence of the Lord (Acts 3:21). Now that is revival!

Dr. David Bryant, of Prayer Concerts International, raised this question at a Pastors' Prayer Summit. What is most on the heart of God? Answer: The glorious revelation of His Son Jesus to the nations of the world! "The Lord will lay bare his holy arm in the sight of all the nations and all the ends of the earth will see the salvation of our God" (Isaiah 52:10). And how does God do this? Through revival! And how does revival come? Through the outpouring of the Holy Spirit in answer to the prayers of the people of God!

When revival was sweeping through Wales in 1904, a man who visited one of the meetings stood up and said, "Friends, I have journeyed into Wales with the hope that I may glean the secret of the Welsh revival." Instantly Evan Roberts, the leader of the revival, was on his feet, and with an uplifted arm toward the speaker, replied, "My brother, there is no secret. Ask and ye shall receive!"

Notes

" … And offered them up upon the altar
for a whole homage offering."
Genesis 8:20, The Septuagint

Chapter 24

ARE YOU 20 MINUTES THANKFUL?

You've heard it said that "time is money." Yes it can be, but time is far more than money. Time is God's gift to us, and how we use it is our gift to Him.

Time. Twenty minutes. Will you give twenty-minutes of your time? Each day? Every day? Until you take your last breath?

Let me explain. The Sunday morning worship service had come to a close. I had just preached a sermon on "Never Miss An Opportunity To Pray" (see Chapter 17). The major point of personal application was asking the congregation, young and old, to make a commitment to pray twenty minutes a day. Everyday. No exceptions. No excuses. No escape. From the written responses turned in, a good number made the commitment to pray.

After the service, we turned our attention to the Sunday School hour. Mark Palmer, one of our mature adult members, was taking his class through a survey of the Old Testament. The lesson that day was in the book of Genesis. He was teaching out of Chapter 8 where Noah came out of the ark after the floodwaters had receded. He pointed out that the first thing Noah did upon disembarking was not to kneel down and kiss the ground, but to look up to God in heaven in worship and prayer. In fact, Noah was so thankful to God for safe passage that he built an altar to the Lord offering sacrifices upon it.

Then, in a masterful teaching stroke linking the sermon we had just heard with his Bible lesson, he paused momentarily and said to the class, "You can see how thankful Noah was. How thankful are you? Are you twenty minutes thankful?"

I was sitting in his class at the time. His words pierced my heart. My own message, phrased somewhat differently, now became eminently practical. Is your gratitude towards God such that you would be willing to spend twenty minutes with Him every day telling Him so?

One of the things I love so much about preaching is that you get the sermon applied twice: once in its preparation, and then again in its delivery. On this day I got it three times! That experience has left an indelible impression on me.

Dear reader, you are just a few pages away from the most important page in this book. If you have not already 'sneaked a peek,' prepare yourself. If you are willing to yield to the opportunity that is soon to be set before you, you are in store for an experience that has the power to change your life forever! Read on!

Notes

"Jesus told them a story showing that it was necessary for them to pray consistently and never quit."
Luke 18:1, The Message

Chapter 25

MAKING THE COMMITMENT TO PRAY

E.M. Bounds, a prolific writer on the subject of prayer said it, I think, best of all. "What the Church needs today is not more or better machinery, not new organizations or more and novel methods, but men whom the Holy Ghost can use ... men of prayer, men mighty in prayer. The Holy Ghost does not flow through methods, but through men. He does not come on machinery, but on men. He does not anoint plans, but men - men of prayer." I might add, women and children of prayer, too.

Which brings us now to you. Take an honest look at yourself. Go stand in front of a mirror and ask yourself this question. "Am I a man, a woman, a child of prayer?" Go ahead. I'll wait for you. Are you? If not, why not? Don't rationalize. Don't make excuses. Would you like to express your devotion to the Lord by being committed to prayer? Yes? I thought you might!

Having come this far in your reading and understanding of the supreme importance of prayer, would you be willing right now to commit yourself to God for 20 minutes in prayer each and every day? Before you make this commitment, please understand that it is not trying harder that will bring about the desired change that you seek in your life. Rather, it is a full and free abandonment to the fullness of Jesus Christ. In making this commitment to pray you are, in fact, yielding, surrendering, and abandoning yourself to Jesus Christ, so that you might experience Him in a fresh, new way. You will have to call upon God, depend on God on a daily basis, if you are to follow through with the commitment to pray. It is not enough here to commit yourself to do the right thing – pray daily. Making the commitment alone to pray will not carry you through. Only a helpless dependence on the Spirit of God at work in you will see you through.

Here is your personally signed and dated commitment to Jesus Christ to pray 20 minutes every day. I've also added two other signature lines for witnesses. I would suggest that you sign this in their presence and ask them to hold you accountable to the commitment you are making.

MY PERSONAL COMMITMENT TO PRAYER

With God as my helper, I commit to pray 20 minutes a day, each and every day.

SIGNED: _____ Date: _____

Witness: _____ Witness: _____

You will discover that as you continue in this discipline of prayer for one month, you will have gone a long way in establishing this spiritual habit for life.

On a practical note: If you find it difficult to get up twenty minutes earlier to pray in the morning, then consider going to bed twenty minutes earlier at night. It works, but you must discipline yourself to do it.

I don't know your life, your schedule, or its demands. I don't know if you're a single parent or if you're working one job, two jobs, or more. But what I do know is that if you set your heart to seek the Lord for at least 20 minutes every day, He will honor your commitment and make a way for you.

Here are just a few suggestions of where you can find twenty minutes every day:

1. Give up one half-hour of television.
2. Spend less time on non-essential phone talk.
3. Don't read 'pop culture' magazines.
4. Ask someone in your family to cover for you (protect your time) while you pray.
5. Pray "first thing" in the morning before others get up and the phone starts ringing.
6. Take your shower, set out your clothes and make your lunch the night before.

7. Get up twenty minutes earlier than usual in the morning.
8. Pray during your lunch hour, if at all possible.
9. Ask God in prayer where you can consistently find twenty minutes a day to pray.

If you've made this commitment to God to pray, may I ask one more thing of you? Would you write to me at the address on page 2 of this book and let me know of your commitment? If you will, here's what I'll do for you. Once a day for 30 days I'll bring your name before the Lord in prayer asking Him to encourage and strengthen you as you walk with Him, and thus enabling you to fulfill your promise to God.

If you find it hard to pray at first, confess the sin of prayerlessness. The answer to prayerlessness is prayer! If you still find it difficult to pray, just spend your time praising God (i.e. pray the Psalms) and soon your prayers will follow.

Dear reader, making the commitment to pray is an important matter. Unless you make a deliberate decision to pray daily, you'll not take care of what's really big in your life. This is so plainly demonstrated in the following story.

One day an expert in time management was speaking to a group of business students and, to drive home a point, used an illustration those students will never forget. As he stood in front of the group of high-powered overachievers, he said, "Okay, time for a quiz." Then he pulled out a one-gallon, wide-mouthed Mason jar and set it on the table in front of him. Next he produced about a dozen fist-sized rocks and carefully placed them, one at a time, into the jar. When the jar was filled to the top and no more rocks would fit inside, he asked, "Is this jar full?"

Everyone in the class said, "Yes."

"Really?" he said. He reached under the table and pulled out a bucket of gravel. Then he dumped some gravel in and shook the jar, causing pieces of gravel to work themselves down into the space between the big rocks. Then he asked the group once more, "Is the jar full?"

By this time the class was on to him. "Probably not," one of them answered.

"Good!" he replied. He reached under the table and brought out a bucket of sand. He started dumping the sand in the jar and it went into all of the spaces left between the rocks and the gravel. Once more he asked the question, "Is this jar full?"

"No!" the class shouted.

Once again, he said, "Good." Then he grabbed a pitcher of water and began to pour it in until the jar was filled to the brim. Then he looked at the class and asked, "What is the point of this illustration?"

One eager beaver raised his hand and said, "The point is, no matter how full your schedule is, if you try really hard, you can always fit some more things in it!"

"No," the speaker replied, "that's not the point. The truth this illustration teaches us is: If you don't put the big rocks in first, you'll never get them in at all."

Let that first big rock be your personal commitment to daily prayer.

Notes

"Could you not keep watch one hour?"
Mark 14:37, The Centenary Translation

Chapter 26

THE POWER OF AN HOUR

What is it?
    Believe it
        Or don't believe it
    You have it
        And I have it
        We all have it
            You can ask for it
                And get it
            Though you had it
                When you requested it
                And when given it
                    You have no more of it
                Than you had of it
                    When you asked for it
    You can give it
        And you can take it
    You can do it
        And you can hear it
        And see it
            You can spend it
                And sell it
            Buy it
                And if you sell it
                    You still have all of it
                And if you buy it
                    You have no more of it
                Than you had of it
                    Before you purchased it

You can use it
And abuse it
You can lose it
And still have it
You can waste it
Yet use all of it
And want more of it
But can't get it.
WHAT IS IT?

The answer is TIME!

Recently, I came across the following illustration. "Imagine there is a bank that credits your account each morning with $86,400. It carries over no balance from day to day, allows you to keep no cash balance, and every evening cancels whatever part of the amount you had failed to use during the day.

What would you do? Draw out every cent, of course! Well, everyone has such a bank. Its name is TIME. Every morning it credits you with 86,400 seconds. Every night it writes off, as lost, whatever of this you have failed to invest to good purpose. It carries over no balance. It allows no overdraft. Each day it opens a new account for you. Each night it burns the remains of the day.

If you fail to use the day's deposits, the loss is yours. There is no going back. There is no drawing against the morrow. You must live in the present on today's deposit. Invest it so as to get from it the utmost in health, happiness and success! The clock is running. Make the most of today.

To realize the value of ONE WEEK, ask an editor of a weekly newspaper. To realize the value of ONE DAY, ask a daily wage laborer who has kids to feed. To realize the value of ONE HOUR, ask the lovers who are waiting to meet. To realize the value of ONE MINUTE, ask a person who has missed the train. To realize the value of ONE SECOND, ask a person who has avoided an accident. To realize the value of ONE MILLISECOND, ask the person who has won a silver medal in the Olympics.

Treasure every moment that you have! And treasure it more because you shared it with someone special, special enough to have your time ... and remember, time waits for no one ...

Yesterday is history

Tomorrow a mystery

Today is a gift

That's why it's called the present!"

Time. Time spent in prayer. You have made, I trust, the commitment to pray everyday for 20 minutes. Now, I wish for you to consider spending some extended time in prayer once a week. To be precise, an hour spent in extended prayer!

In the closing hours of Jesus' earthly life we come to a most critical hour. It takes place in the Garden of Gethsemane (Mark 14:32-42):

"They went to a place called Gethsemane, and Jesus said to his disciples, "Sit here while I pray." He took Peter, James and John along with him, and he began to be deeply distressed and troubled. "My soul is overwhelmed with sorrow to the point of death," he said to them. "Stay here and keep watch."

Going a little farther, he fell to the ground and prayed that if possible the hour might pass from him. "Abba, Father," he said, "everything is possible for you. Take this cup from me. Yet not what I will, but what you will."

Then he returned to his disciples and found them sleeping. "Simon," he said to Peter, "are you asleep? Could you not keep watch for one hour? Watch and pray so that you will not fall into temptation. The spirit is willing, but the body is weak."

Once more he went away and prayed the same thing. When he came back, he again found them sleeping, because their eyes were heavy. They did not know what to say to him.

Returning the third time, he said to them, "Are you still sleeping and resting? Enough! The hour has come. Look! The Son of Man is betrayed into the hands of sinners. Rise! Let us go! Here comes my betrayer!"

Gethsemane in the Hebrew language means "oil press," (i.e., a place for squeezing the oil from olives). However, something far more precious was being squeezed that dark night ... blood sweat. The historian Luke wrote, "And being in anguish, he prayed more earnestly, and his sweat was like drops of blood falling to the ground" (Luke 22:44). It was here that our Lord agonized in prayer. Knowing full well the unbounded horror and suffering that lay before him, Jesus prayed to the Father. He prayed that, if possible, the approaching hour of sorrow might pass from him. "Nevertheless," he said, "I yield, Father, to your will in this matter." Jesus prayed like this for one hour.

Upon returning to his disciples, he found them asleep. Asleep on the job. Asleep at the wheel. Asleep on their watch. Our Lord addresses Peter. "Are you asleep? Could you not keep watch for one hour? Watch and pray so that you will not fall into temptation. The spirit is willing, but the body is weak" (Mark 14:37-38). Note: Although Jesus asked for one hour, He himself gave more, going back a second and third time!

Jesus singled Peter out because of his bold assertion that he would not fail. Earlier that same evening Jesus had said, "You will all fall away." Peter declared, "Even if all fall away, I will not." He went on to insist emphatically, "Even if I have to die with you, I will never disown you" (Mark 14:29-31). Not deny you! Not disown you! How about staying awake in prayer for just one hour, Peter?

This is serious business. Let me ask you a few questions. Are you asleep? Can you keep watch for one hour? Have you gone to sleep on Jesus? Are you willing to go without sleep for Jesus? Can you stick it out with Jesus for a single hour?

God gives to everyone the same amount of time. What we do with it is up to us. He gives us one hundred and sixty-eight hours every week, no more and no less, just like clockwork. Can't we give him back one hour of extended praying once a week?

The exhortation to pray for one hour is for our spiritual benefit. Our Lord Jesus is saying, in effect, watch and pray so that when the hour of trial comes you won't break down. Stay alert so you don't enter the danger zone unknowingly. When there is physical danger, we're on the alert. Do we not understand spiritual danger? There are, in fact, evil forces at work opposing us. There is the temptation to be unfaithful to Jesus when things threaten us. The way to deal with that temptation is to watch and pray. You defeat the tempter (the devil) by being loyal to Jesus. As you stand firm in the faith, engaged in prayer, you will be victorious (see I Peter 5:6-11; Revelation 2:10).

Our commitment to Christ may be quite sincere, but the problem is that we are vulnerable and weak if left to ourselves. We have a willing spirit but weak body. And that is why we must pray. As one writer put it, "Part of you is eager for anything in God, but another part is as lazy as an old dog sleeping by the fire."

I have always been singularly impressed with the Moravian church and their devotion to prayer expressed in the "Hourly Intercession," or prayer watch. The Moravian church is a mainstream Reformed Protestant church that began in the 15th century in Moravia and Bohemia. It has a worldwide membership of about 500,000 of which 60,000 are to be found in North America.

The Moravians worked out a schedule so that some of their church members would always be praying, every hour of the day and night. One man and one woman were assigned to watch and pray. This prayer watch continued for over one hundred years without interruption! As someone has said, it was "the longest prayer meeting on record."

The Scripture says, "There is a time for everything and a season for every activity under heaven" (Ecclesiastes 3:1). There is a time for sleeping and a time for praying. Like the disciples, we are without excuse (Mark 14:41).

To illustrate the power of *extended praying* I relate this story I heard told by the Rev. Dick Kaufmann, a Presbyterian pastor in New York City. Pastor Kaufmann was asked to preside at a funeral. At the viewing the night before the service, a woman unknown to him sought him out for some inexplicable reason and, whispering in his ear, said, "The Christians had their night tonight, but tomorrow is our day!" Without revealing his identity, he discovered the woman to be a Druid. She considered herself to be a member of the ancient Celtic priesthood of magicians and wizards.

At this juncture, let me hasten to add that Pastor Kaufmann believes that recruiting prayer partners is one of the most significant things that you can do. And recruit he did. The word went out, asking for extended praying for the service the next day. There were many who exchanged sleep for prayer that night.

Morning broke. At the burial site, Rev. Kaufmann stood at one end of the casket, the Druid woman at the other. The lines were drawn. The battle would soon ensue. As Pastor Kaufmann began to preach he enjoyed what he said later was an uncommon liberty in declaring the good news of the gospel.

After the service was concluded, Pastor Kaufmann's wife approached him and said in amazement, "How did you ever manage to speak with such freedom and power while the whole time that you were preaching the Druid woman kept shaking her head No! No! No! to everything you said.

Pastor Kaufmann replied to his wife that all he saw was the woman's head going up and down Yes! Yes! Yes! Oh, the power of an hour spent in prayer! Oh, the pleasure of prayer – the pleasure of spending an hour in the company of Jesus!

Which brings us now to our point of personal application. Would you be willing to spend one hour once a week in extended prayer? Your twenty minutes for that one day would be expanded to 60 minutes. You may find it convenient to do this on a Sunday afternoon while others in your household are resting or are otherwise engaged.

Putting this all together, if you spend twenty minutes a day praying for six days, you will have prayed for two hours. When you add in the one hour of praying on your seventh day, you will have prayed that week for three hours. If you multiply your three hours by 52 weeks in a year you will have prayed 156 hours, or almost the equivalent of an entire week day and night spent in prayer to God.

Although the value of prayer is not to be judged solely by the amount of time spent doing it, there can be no doubt that the more time you spend with God, the more you will grow in your relationship with Him, and the more you will see your prayers answered!

Does all this praying sound ambitious to you? Absolutely. But is this not God's ambition for us?

"Could you not keep watch for one hour?"

- Jesus

Your spirit is willing. The Spirit wills it. You can do it. Commit yourself to Jesus Christ to do it. Rely wholly upon the Spirit at work in you, giving you both the desire and the power to do it! (Philippians 2:13)

"The smoke of incense ascended,
with the prayers of Christ's people,
from the hand of the angel before God."
Revelation 8:4, Twentieth Century New Testament

Chapter 27

BUILDING A LIFE OF PRAYER
(Five Steps to Building a Life of Prayer)

Motivational speaker Carett Robert once said, "You can't get up there and insult (an audience) by trying to tell them how to run their life or operate their business. You just try to help them along. It's like the best prayer I ever heard. 'Dear God, please help me be the person my dog thinks I am.'" Of course, when it comes right down to it, what matters the most is not what you think or I think or someone else thinks, it's what God thinks.

What God thinks as revealed in Scripture is that prayer is pleasing to Him. The prayers of the saints are like a sweet aroma, wafting upward toward God in heaven. "The smoke of the incense, together with the prayers of the saints, went up before God from the angel's hand" (Revelation 8:4).

Our prayer life is to be a life of sweet, cherished intimacy with the Lord. After all, what is it that we were created for? God made us for His glory so that we might spend an eternity in the worship and fellowship of himself. And whatever heaven is like, it's got to be far greater than what we know here. This desire for intimacy with the Lord reminds me of the young man who went to the top of a mountain and shouted out, "I want more of you." And the echo overwhelmed him when he heard, "I WANT MORE OF YOU!" Does that describe you? Do you want more of God? Then he'll demand more of you.

So, in a real spiritual sense, prayer is fitting us out for heaven. When faith shall be changed to sight, when we see Jesus face-to-face, our prayers will give way to praise. Prayers will be needed no more. Praise will be the language of heaven. The hallelujah chorus will be the chosen hymn of heaven!

We turn our attention now to five steps for building a life of prayer. And as you would do in any building project, we'll approach this in an orderly and progressive way.

Step Number One: Be Consistent

Our prayers are to be daily prayers. Jesus underscored this when he taught his disciples to pray, "Give us *each day* our daily bread" (Luke 11:3). God arranged it this way so that we would keep coming back to him day after day after day. Every day when we sit down to eat we can give thanks to God for the meal provided, for this is surely in answer to our prayers. We are to pray day in and day out. Consistency is key here. It will, of course, require daily discipline on your part.

This kind of consistency was evident in the life of the Apostle Paul. In writing to the young pastor, Timothy, he said: "I thank God, whom I serve, as my forefathers did, with a clear conscience, as *night and day* I *constantly* remember you in my prayers" (II Timothy 1:3). See also Romans 1:9-10; Colossians 1:9.

Step Number Two: Be Persistent

Nowhere in Scripture is persistence in prayer better exemplified than in the parable our Lord taught about the 'Persistent Widow,' or perhaps better yet, the pestering widow. The parable was taught to the disciples "to show them that they should always pray and not give up" (Luke 18:1).

When our prayers are not immediately answered, we are not to give up or give in; give up in our praying or give in to doubt, fear, discouragement, etc. Always refuse to give up or give in, except to the will of God.

In the parable a widow sought out the local judge, demanding justice because of her opponent. She continued to harass the judge to the point that he realized that unless he met her demand, she would never go away. When the Scripture uses the words 'wear me out' (verse 5), it means to hit under the eye or to beat black and blue. Figuratively, then, it means to weary someone into compliance. So to get some peace for himself, he granted her request.

Now the point of the story is this. If this is what a helpless widow could secure for herself from a 'I don't care about God or man' judge, how much more will God see to it that his children receive what they need through persistence in prayer.

Step Number Three: Be Resistant

Jesus Christ bought the right for you to get an answer to your prayers. So you must resist and rebuke all opposition that comes your way. Your greatest enemy here is the devil himself. Satan comes only to steal, kill, and destroy. The devil will do everything in his limited but brutal power to keep you from praying. You must resist him. James said, "Resist the devil and he will flee from you" (James 4:7). Peter tells us how to do this. "Be self-controlled and alert. Your enemy the devil prowls around like a roaring lion looking for someone to devour. Resist him, standing firm in the faith" (I Peter 5:8-9). We are told to flee from sexual immorality, from idolatry and from the evil desires of youth, but never to flee from the devil. The devil is to flee from us when we resist him by standing our ground in the faith, by holding fast to what we know to be true.

Step Number Four: Be Expectant

"In the morning, O Lord, you hear my voice, in the morning I lay my requests before you and *wait in expectation*" (Psalm 5:3). Or as Habakkuk stated it so succinctly, "I will stand at my watch and station myself on the ramparts; I will look to see what he will say to me" (Habakkuk 2:1). When we pray we should expect God to reply because He is a God who hears and answers our prayers (Psalm 116:1-2; Psalm 120:1).

Step Number Five: Be Patient

Consistent, Persistent, Resistant, Expectant, and now, finally, Patient. Patience is saved for last because it is the one who waits patiently who is rewarded. Sometimes God is quick to answer, but when he is not, we must be patient. As an example of patience, consider the prophets. "Take the old prophets as your mentors. They put up with anything, went through everything, and never once quit, all the time honoring God. What a gift of life to those who stay the course! You've heard, of course, of Job's staying power, and you know how God brought it all together for him at the end. That's because God cares, cares right down to the last detail" (James 5:10-11, The Message).

"Jehovah will hear when I call unto him."
Psalm 4:3, The American Standard Version

Chapter 28

A HOUSE OF PRAYER

"Wherever God erects a house of prayer,
The Devil always builds a chapel there;
And 'twill be found, upon examination
The latter has the largest congregation."
— Daniel Defoe

In Mark 11:12-16 Jesus uses the cursing of the fig tree and the cleaning of the Temple as an opportunity to teach his disciples about prayer. The two stories were never intended to stand alone, but are in fact related. In linking these two events, Jesus speaks, first of all, about the impending judgment of God upon Israel and then about the power of faith operating through prayer. We shall see how these two meet head on as the story progresses.

"The next day as they were leaving Bethany, Jesus was hungry. Seeing in the distance a fig tree in leaf, he went to find out if it had any fruit. When he reached it, he found nothing but leaves, because it was not the season for figs. Then he said to the tree, "May no one ever eat fruit from you again." And his disciples heard him say it. On reaching Jerusalem, Jesus entered the temple area and began driving out those who were buying and selling there. He overturned the tables of the moneychangers and the benches of those selling doves, and would not allow anyone to carry merchandise through the temple courts" (Mark 11:12-16).

Although it was not the season for fruit in Palestine because there were leaves on the tree, Jesus, upon inspection, rightly expected to find fruit. Instead, he found nothing but leaves. And so he cursed the fig tree, saying, "May no one ever eat fruit from you again" (Mark 11:14).

What our Lord condemns here is all show but no substance. There was foliage, but no fruit. Jesus, in a natural or physical sense, is looking to satisfy his hunger. In a spiritual sense, he is desirous of finding fruit in us, fruitful living.

In Scripture, Israel is often portrayed as a fig tree. The curse of Jesus came as a prophetic warning to Israel: "Produce fruit in keeping with repentance" (Luke 3:8) or else! Or else what? Or else divine judgment will fall upon you.

It is necessary that we relate the withered tree to what the disciples saw that very day in the Temple. There was all this frenzied activity of buying, selling, sheep bleating, wings of doves flapping, shoppers and merchants haggling, and coins clinking. Our Lord begins his day's work by cleaning house.

Now the relation between these two events comes into clear focus. As there was no fruit on the tree, so there was no life (spiritual) in the Temple. And so, we have a fruitless fig tree and a lifeless Temple; a temple area devoid of the manifest presence of God. Rather than the sweet fragrance of prayer rising up to God there is the stench of manure; *offal* rather than *offering*.

Jesus seized the moment to bring a lesson from God. He taught them, saying, "Is it not written: My house will be called a house of prayer for all nations? But you have made it a den of robbers!" (Mark 11:17).

Our Lord's teaching centered around Isaiah 56:7 with a reference also to Jeremiah 7:11. In context, Isaiah 56:3-7 speaks of the future coming of godly foreigners (Gentiles) to the Temple for prayer and sacrifice. It also defines for us what prayer is. To pray is "to love the name of the Lord and to worship Him" (Isaiah 56:6). And then, too, prayer is a way of approaching God for the cleaning of your house (life); the cleansing of your soul.

The Lord's house is first and foremost a house of prayer. Jesus refers to the Temple as "my house." When you come to worship, it is his Name that is over the door. And he means for it to be a place of prayer *"for all nations."* The church of the living God is to be inclusive; it is for both Jew and Gentile.

Now what do you do when you go to someone else's house? You observe their customs. You follow their rules. Jesus meant for us to pray when we come to his house.

After the cleansing of the Temple, Jesus used the incident of the withered fig tree as an opportunity to explain the power of faith and prayer. He told his disciples that they must have a faith that rests on God. He also spoke of the power of faith through prayer in the face of impossible situations.

George Mueller operated an orphanage in Bristol, England on the basis of prayer. Prayers of thanksgiving were offered to God for the food when there was not a crumb on the table. Food was always provided in response to prayer – a meal was never missed!

As we make our way to church each week, the worship of God through prayer ought to be uppermost in our minds. As important as all the other elements of worship are (e.g. Scripture, sermon, sacrament, song, etc.), Jesus singled out prayer. His desire is to hear our voice raised in prayers of praise and thanksgiving. After all, if it were not for God, we would have no one to thank and nothing to give.

"Steady then, keep cool and pray.
I Peter 4:7, The Moffatt Translation

Chapter 29

PRAYER AND THE NEW MILLENNIUM

There was a sign in a coat shop in London that said: "We have been in business 103 years. We have survived depressions, wars, recessions and times of prosperity. We have been robbed, swindled, broken into, burned and generally frustrated. We have had prosperous times and lean times. We have faced bankruptcy. We have made good profits. We remain open because we wouldn't want to miss what happens next." - Attributed to Brad Curl

What's next for us? The Apostle Peter wrote about it. "The end of all things is near. Therefore, be clear minded and self-controlled *so that you can pray*" (I Peter 4:7).

We are to be clear-minded (thought) and self-controlled (deed) so that we can pray (word). As the new millennium has arrived, as Armageddon approaches, as we wait to welcome a new heaven and a new earth (Revelation 21:1), the Bible says that we are to focus on prayer. As the return of our Lord draws near, only eternity will reveal what God was pleased to accomplish through our prayers.

I am reminded of a story that I once heard on the radio. A man stood on the dock watching the arrival of a luxurious cruise ship. A brass band was playing ... streamers were flying ... people were waving and shouting. It seemed clear that some celebrity was on board and was receiving a royal welcome home.

Our friend who had suffered much and lived on little in the service of Jesus began to wonder. And then, speaking to the Lord, he said, "Lord, I've been faithful in your service all these years, devoted to you in prayer all my life and I've never had such a welcome." Then this thought was whispered to his heart,

"My son, you will, for you see, you've not yet come home!" Home to your reward. Home to heaven!

Devotion to prayer is devotion to Jesus. It's everything from A to Z, from adoration to zeal. It will be worth it all when we see Jesus.

There is a Chinese saying that ...

"If you want one year of prosperity, grow grain

If you want 10 years of prosperity, grow trees

If you want 100 years of prosperity, grow people."

God is in the business of growing people, of growing them to maturity. The gift of prayer is one of the gracious means he uses so that, when we do grow up, we'll be just like Jesus. After all, isn't that what being a Christian is all about?

Notes

**"For everyone who calls upon the name of
the Lord will be saved."
Romans 10:13, The Williams Translation**

Chapter 30

A PILGRIM'S PROGRESS

"Generous in love – God, give grace!
Huge in mercy – wipe out my bad record.
Scrub away my guilt ... soak me in your laundry and I'll
    come out clean"
                            (Psalm 51:1-2, 7, The Message).

Before I became a Christian, my life was riddled with guilt; the guilt of my sins. I woke up every morning feeling guilty. At night as I lay down, even then, my guilt would cover me like a blanket. I felt guilty the few times I went to church, and I felt guilty when I didn't. Guilt was my unwelcome companion.

Then I met a Person who changed my life forever. His name ... Jesus. Here's how it happened. My sister, Judi, who is a year older than I, had become a Christian in her mid-teens through the witness of her boyfriend. After that she would retreat most every evening to our hall closet to pray. Seated on a small chair, surrounded by hanging coats and dangling umbrellas, Judi would plead with God for the salvation of her family. As I lay in my bed I could hear her muffled cry, "Oh God, save Johnny. Oh God, save Johnny." This nightly ritual continued for many months, stretching out to over a year.

And then, one summer's eve, God chose to graciously answer a young girl's prayer. At the invitation of my sister, I attended an evangelistic service at a local church. It pleased God, as I sat under the preaching of the gospel of Jesus Christ, to grant me the faith to believe in Him and the desire to turn away from my sin. I did. In fact, on that very night I trusted in Jesus Christ alone for my eternal salvation. Grace appeared, guilt disappeared. Jesus not only took away *the guilt* of my sin; he forgave me for all my sins!

I owed a debt I could not pay. Jesus paid a debt he did not owe. How can I ever repay Jesus? I can't. But there is one thing I can do. I can show Jesus just how very grateful I am by living for him and no longer for myself. That, by the grace of God, is just what I'm seeking to do.

It all comes back to grace. You're either in grace or disgrace. I like it right here in grace. Grace is the place for me!

As you turn now to the last chapter of this book, you, too, can experience the life-changing power of the risen Christ.

Notes

"Whoever has faith may have in
him (Jesus) eternal life."
John 3:15, The New Testament in Basic English

Chapter 31

IT'S A WONDERFUL LIFE

Dear reader, in many respects this closing chapter is the most important chapter of all. If you have never offered the prayer, or one like it, toward the close of this chapter, I urge you to thoughtfully and sincerely do so. "For *everyone who calls* on the name of the Lord will be saved" (Romans 10:13).

Let's begin, then, with a question. Is your life wonderful or do you just wonder about life?

The Christian life is a wonderful life. Where else can you know:

- Acceptance by God into the warmth of His unfailing love
- The forgiveness of your sins – all of them
- The peace of God which quiets the troubled soul
- A God who fills your heart with great joy
- The Lord's purpose for your life
- The assurance of eternal life

And who is it that makes life so wonderful? The answer is to be found in a name ...Jesus Christ. Jesus means, "the Lord is salvation." Christ means "the Anointed One." Jesus Christ then is the one anointed (or chosen) by God to save us from our sins. The Bible declares, "Jesus is the only One who can save people. His name is the only power in the world that has been given to save people. We must be saved through him" (Acts 4:12).

In order to save sinners, it was necessary that Christ should be both God and man. It was only as sinless man that Jesus could be our substitute on the cross and take the punishment for our sins. It was only as God that Christ could give his sacrifice infinite value and bear the wrath of God so that we might be delivered from it. God has given proof to people everywhere that

He accepts the death of Jesus as the payment for our sins by raising him from the dead. As the Scripture says, "He (Jesus) is able always to save those who come to God through him because he always lives, asking God to help them" (Hebrews 7:25).

Now at this point you may be thinking, "How can I come into this wonderful life in Jesus Christ?" Again, the Bible gives the answer. "(We) must turn to God in repentance and have faith in our Lord Jesus" (Acts 20:21). Repentance means a change of mind, leading to a change in your personal behavior. It means that you stop doing the wrong you've been doing. It involves turning to God to do what is right in His eyes and turning away from what God says is sinful and wrong. Faith in the Lord Jesus means that you put your trust in Jesus Christ alone to save you from your sins. All of this means that you are committing your life to Jesus Christ as your Savior and Lord. He is the One of whom the Scripture says, "A child has been born to us, God has given a son to us. He will be responsible for leading people. His name will be *Wonderful* Counselor, Powerful God, Father Who Lives Forever, Prince of Peace" (Isaiah 9:6).

You may wish to use the following prayer to express your need for Jesus Christ.

Dear God, be merciful to me the sinner that I am. I believe that your Son, Jesus Christ, died for all my sins and rose again to live forever. I turn to you and I turn away from my sins to serve you, the living and true God. Come live in me, Lord Jesus Christ. In your name I pray. Amen.

If you pray to receive Jesus Christ into your life, then you have this personal assurance from the Bible. "To all who did accept him (Jesus) and believe in him he (God) gave the right to become children of God. They did not become his children in any human way – by human parents or human desire. They were born of God" (John 1:12-13).

As you begin your new, *wonderful life* in Christ you will want to do the following:

- Read and study your Bible as often as you can (Ezra 7:10).
- Pray about everything (Philippians 4:6-7).

- Live and be led by the Holy Spirit into holy living (Galatians 5:13-26).
- Attend a church where the Bible is taught and Jesus is worshipped as Savior and Lord (Matthew 28:9).
- Tell your family and friends and the one who gave you this book what wonderful things the Lord has done for you and how he has had mercy on you (Mark 5:19-20).

In closing, I share with you a startling story of a young man who committed his life to Jesus Christ and the amazing result that followed.

A young man who had been raised as an atheist was training to be an Olympic diver. The only religious influence in his life came from an outspoken Christian friend. The young diver never really paid much attention to his friend's messages, but he heard them often.

One night the diver went to the indoor pool at the college he attended. The lights were all off, but as the pool had big skylights and the moon was bright, there was plenty of light to practice by. The young man climbed up to the highest diving board, and as he turned his back to the pool on the edge of the board and extended his arms out, he saw his shadow on the wall. The shadow of his body was in the shape of a cross. Instead of diving, he knelt down in prayer and asked Jesus Christ to come into his life. As the young man stood, a maintenance man walked in and turned the lights on. The pool had been drained for repairs.

The most important thing you can do right now is to pray. Would you kneel down right now and simply but sincerely ask Jesus Christ to come into your life? As you do so, you can be assured of the following: "God has given us eternal life, and this life is in his Son. He who has the Son has life" (I John 5:11-12). It's just that simple. The life you are looking for is found in Jesus.

Let me be among the first to say to you, "Welcome to the family of God!"

With Grace and Gratitude,
John Evans